ISLE OF MAN

WRITTEN AND EDITED BY ANDREW DOUGLAS

CONTENTS

Foreword	2
Welcome	4
Manx	5
Bienvenu	5
Welkom	6
Willkommen	6
One Man's Man	9
The Island's History	18
Coasts and Islands	24
Mountains, Valleys, Glens and Parks	31
Sheadings and Parishes	34
Travelling to the Isle of Man	35
Towns and Villages	38
Beaches, Leisure and Entertainment Guide	100
Days Out by Car	108
Getting around the Island	136
Museums of Mann	141
Legends of Mann	146
Accommodation & Eating Out	152
Index and Acknowledgments	189
Discount Vouchers	189

MAPS

The Isle of Man	8
Sheadings and Parishes	34

THE TOWNS AND VILLAGES

Castletown	61
Douglas	40
Onchan	97
Peel	77
Port Erin & Port St. Mary	65
Ramsey	88

© Copyright 1994s Lily Publications (Isle of Man). All rights reserved. Any reproduction in whole or in part is strictly prohibited. The content contained herein is based on the best available information at the time of research. The publishers assume no liability whatsoever arising from the publishing of material contained herein.

Published by Lily Publications (Isle of Man), PO Box 1,
Portland House, Station Road, Ballasalla, Isle of Man. Tel: (0646) 823644

Head Office: Lily Publications, 12 Millfields Close,
Pentlepoir, Kilgetty, Pembrokeshire, Wales SA68 0SA.
Tel: (0834) 811895
Fax: (0834) 814484
ISBN 0 9517868 9 X

FOREWORD

It was with the greatest of pleasure that I accepted the invitation to write the foreword to the Lily Isle of Man 1994/5 Guide. My Department has recognised the value to our industry of such a publication and have no hesitation in recommending it to you.

The Isle of Man is a land rich in tradition and culture and as it faces up to the next millenium, so the telling of its story will grow in importance. It is a story that is a tapestry of events, rich in drama and yet throughout all the upheavals, it is a tale of human endeavour.

It is a country with a vide variety of scenery reminding visitors of almost every corner of the British Isles; with heather covered hills, steep glens, lush fields, near vertical cliffs, castles, parks and yet with a taste and flavour of its own. Transportation on the Island offers the tourist a chance to travel by steam or electric trains and Douglas has the unique horse trams to carry you from one end of the Bay to the other. Events and attractions are plentiful during the year. With the oldest continuous form of government in the world we have a

stability and a quality of life that is much admired by visitors to our shores. The relaxed way of life on our Island is probably best summed up in the Manx expression "Traady-liooar", translating as time enough.

However equally important as our scenic and other attractions is the warm hospitality that the Manx people show our visitors. Ours is a land of friendly people, eager to make you welcome. I hope you will find time enough to visit us.

Hon Allan R Bell, MHK
Minister
Isle of Man Department of Tourism, Leisure and Transport

Port St. Mary

WELCOME

THE ISLE OF MAN – BRITAIN'S TREASURED ISLAND – AN INTRODUCTION

Since time immemorial the Isle of Man has offered to its visitors a glimpse of all that was good in the past, blended with a sense of anticipation of what the future might hold. Small in area, it has always managed to portray its beauty and delights, spreading the message in a manner that has reached every corner of the globe.

Geographically the Isle of Man lies midway between the coasts of England, Ireland, Scotland and Wales – "the adjacent islands". The Island measures at its extremities 33 miles (52kms) by 13 miles (22kms) and has a land mass area of some 227 square miles (572 sq.kms). It offers a wide variety of scenery covering virtually every type found elsewhere in the British Isles, ranging from vast stretches of open moorland, thickly wooded glens, to palm fringed ponds. Encompassed within over 100 miles (160kms) of coastline there is a central range of mountains and hills lying in a North Easterly/South Westerly direction with well defined valleys leading down to rocky cliffs and sheltered bays. This contrasts with the flat Northern plain's lazy rivers and streams meandering down to its long sandy beaches.

The Isle of Man has an equable climate lacking in extremes by virtue of its location and enjoying the warming influence of the Gulf Stream which flows around the shoreline. Prevailing winds blow from the South West, giving varying degrees of shelter and exposure island wide due to the rugged nature of the topography. With the end of winter the improving weather of March and April is proving increasingly attractive to visitors. In summer, the months of May and June are usually the driest whilst May, June and July are the sunniest. July and August are the warmest and more often than not, September and October enjoy fine weather.

In recent years, there has been a growth in the

Castletown

resident population to the present level of some 70,000. This gives a density of just 308 people per square mile (122 per sq.km) and with about 40% of the Island being uninhabited, there is always plenty of room to move around. The major centre of population is based in Douglas, the capital, with approximately 22,000 residents, a further 28,000 live in seven other main towns and villages.

Contained within this green, pleasant and very fertile land are many surprises! The Island has the oldest continuous Parliament in the world, its own currency, stamps, telecommunications, language, castles, legends and customs, and they all come together with lots more to make the Isle of Man... "Britain's Treasured Island". Come on over and see for yourself.

Welcome

FAILT ERRIU
ELLAN VANNIN – YN ELLAN SHIANT –
ROIE-RAA

Neayr's traa erskyn towse, ta Mannin er jebbal da goaldee shilley jeh dy chooilley red va mie ayns ny shenn laghyn, kianlt seose marish roie-ennaghtyn jeh'n traa ry-heet. Ga dy vel ee beg, v'eh rieau cheet lhee dy hoilshaghey magh yn aalid as eunys eck, skeayley magh yn chaghteraght shen dy roshtyn gagh ard jeh'n chruinney.

Ta Ellan Vannin sy vean, eddyr Sostyn, Nerin, Nalbin as Bretin – 'ny hellanyn sniessey'. Ta lhiurid smoo yn Ellan 33 meeiley (52 km) as ta'n lheead smoo 13 meeiley (22 km), as she 227 meeiley kerrinagh (572 km kerr.) yn eaghtyr-thallooin jee. Shimmey reayrt-cheerey ta ry-akin ayns Mannin, goaill stiagh bunnys gagh sorch dy reayrt ta ry-akin ayns Ellanyn Sheear ny hOarpey, goll veih reeastaneyn mooarey gys glionteenyn lesh ymmodee biljyn gys puill chemmit lesh biljyn-palm. Cheu-sthie jeh 100 meeiley (160 km) as ny smoo jeh slyst-marrey, ta dreeym meanagh dy 'leityn as crink ta goll veih'n Chiar-hwoaie gys yn Cheear-ass lesh coanyn coon ta goll sheese dys eayninyn creggagh as baieaghyn fasteeagh. S'mooar yn anchaslys eddyr shen as awinyn as strooanyn litcheragh y thalloo rea twoaie ta goll dy moal dys ny traieyn geinnee liauyrey ayns shen.

Ta emshyr Vannin kenjal dy liooar kyndagh rish y voayl t'ee ayn, as ee goaill soylley jeh chiow y 'Trooan Gulf, ta goll mygeayrt-y-mooee. Ta'n thalloo sleitagh cur fastee ny lhiggey y raad da'n gheay neear-ass, y gheay chliaghtagh. Ta ny turryssee cheet dy choontey ny smoo jeh'n emshyr ayns Mee Vayrnt as Averil, ta sharaghey lurg y geurey. Sy tourey, ta Mee Boaldyn as Mean-souree cliaghtey ve ny meeghyn smoo chirrym, as ta'n emshyr smoo grianagh ayns Mee Boaldyn, Mean-souree as Jerrey-souree. She Jerrey-souree as Luanistyn ny meeghyn s'choe, as, son y chooid smoo, ta emshyr vraew ry-gheddyn ayns Mean-fouyir as Jerrey-fouyir.

Er y gherrid, ta earroo cummaltee Vannin er nirree gys red goll rish 70,000. Ta shen dy ghra, cha nel agh 308 persoonyn ayns gagh meeiley kerrinagh (122 ayns gagh km kerr.). Cha nel sleih cummal ayns 40% jeh'n Ellan, as myr shen ta kinjagh rheamys dy liooar dy gholl mygeayrt ayn. Ta'n chooid smoo jeh ny cummaltee ayns Doolish, yn ard-valley, lesh red goll rish 22,000 cummaltee. Cheu-mooie jeh shen, ta 28,000 dy 'leih cummal ayns shiaght baljyn elley.

Shimmey yindys t'ayns y cheer shoh, ta glass, taitnyssagh as feer hroaragh! Yn ard-whaiyl shinney sy teihll va chaglym gyn scuirr, as ny reddyn elley shoh s'lesh ayns Ellan neesht: yn argid eck hene, ny cowraghyn-postagh, chellinsh, y chengey, cashtallyn, skeealyn as cliaghtaghyn. T'ad ooilley cheet ry-cheilley lesh ram reddyn elley dy yannoo 'Yn Ellan Shiant' ass Mannin. Tar harrish as fow magh dhyt hene.

PRÉSENTATION DE L'ÎLE DE MAN, JOYAU DES ÎLES BRITANNIQUES.
BIENVENUE À TOUS!

Depuis la nuit des temps, visiter l'île de Man c'est découvrir un peu ce qu'il y a eu de bon dans le passé tout en ayant un avant-goût de l'avenir. En dépit de sa petite taille, l'île a su témoigner de sa beauté et de ses merveilles aux quatre coins du monde.

Géographiquement, l'île de Man se trouve à mi-chemin entre les côtes anglaises, irlandaises, écossaises et galloises: les îles environnantes. L'île mesure à ses extrémités 52km sur 22km pour une superficie de 572km_. Elle présente une grande variété de paysages couvrant pratiquement tout ceux que l'on trouve dans les îles Britanniques: de grandes étendues de landes sauvages, des gorges couvertes de forêts denses, des étangs bordés de palmiers. Ceinturée de plus de 160km de côtes, la chaîne centrale de montagnes et de collines, orientée du nord-est au sud-ouest, possède de magnifiques vallées encaissées aboutissant à des falaises rocheuses et des baies abritées. Quel contraste saisissant avec la plaine uniforme du nord où les méandres des rivières et des cours d'eau aboutissent à de grandes plages sablonneuses!

L'île de Man jouit d'un bon climat, sans températures extrêmes, grâce à sa position et à l'influence du Gulf Stream qui réchauffe son littoral. Les vents soufflent principalement du sud-ouest et la nature escarpée du relief donne à cette île de grands contrastes avec des endroits exposés et d'autres abrités. Dès la fin de l'hiver, les visiteurs apprécient déjà l'amélioration progressive du temps au mois de mars et d'avril. En été, les mois de mai et de juin sont généralement les plus secs et mai, juin, juillet les plus ensoleillés. Juillet et août sont les plus doux et très souvent il fait encore beau en septembre et octobre.

Ces dernières années, la population a augmenté pour atteindre actuellement environ 70 000 habitants. Ceci représente une densité de 122 habitants au km_ et comme 40% de l'île est inhabitée, il y a encore beaucoup de place. Une grande partie de la population est concentrée dans la capitale, Douglas, qui compte environ 22 000 habitants, les sept autres villes et villages principaux regroupent 28 000 personnes.

Ce pays verdoyant, plein de charme et extrêmement fertile réserve bien des surprises! L'île a le plus ancien parlement du monde en exercice sans interruption, sa propre monnaie, timbres, télécommunications, langue, châteaux, légendes et coutumes. Il y aurait bien plus à dire sur l'île de Man, le joyau des îles Britanniques, alors il vaut mieux y aller soi-même pour découvrir ses merveilles.

WELKOM
HET EILAND MAN – ENGELAND'S BEST BEWAARDE EILAND – EEN INLEIDING

Sinds onheuglijke tijden heeft het eiland Man zijn bezoekers een vluchtige blik geboden op alles wat goed was in het verleden, vermengd met een voorgevoel van wat de toekomst zou kunnen brengen. Klein in oppervlakte, is het altijd in staat geweest zijn schoonheid en genoegens op zodanige wijze af te schilderen, dat de boodschap over de gehele aarde is verspreid.

Geografisch gezien ligt het eiland Man in het midden tussen de kusten van Engeland, Ierland, Schotland en Wales – "de aangrenzende eilanden". Het eiland meet tussen de uiteinden 33 bij 13 mijl (52 bij 22 km.) en heeft een oppervlakte van ongeveer 227 vierkante mijl (572 vierkante km.). Het biedt een grote verscheidenheid aan natuurschoon met vrijwel elk type dat elders op de Britse Eilanden te vinden is, variërend van uitgestrekte heides en dik beboste bergdalen tot met palmen omzoomde plassen. Omringd door meer dan 100 mijl (160 km.) kustlijn ligt een centraal bergketen in een noordoost/zuidwestelijke richting met duidelijk begrensde valleien die naar steile rotsen en beschutte baaien aflopen. Dit vormt een kontrast met de trage rivieren en stromen die zich van de noordelijke vlakte naar de lange zandstranden aldaar omlaag slingeren.

Het eiland Man heeft een gelijkmatig klimaat zonder uitersten tengevolge van zijn positie binnen de verwarmende invloed van de Golfstroom die langs de kust stroomt. De heersende wind is zuidwestelijk en tengevolge van de ruwe topografie wordt men hier afwisselend tegen beschut en aan blootgesteld. Het beter wordende weer tegen het einde van de winter in maart en april blijkt steeds aantrekkelijker te worden voor bezoekers. In de zomer zijn de maanden mei en juni gewoonlijk het droogst, terwijl mei, juni en juli het zonnigst zijn. Juli en augustus zijn het warmst en meestal is het in september en oktober mooi weer.

In de laatste jaren was er een groei in de vaste bevolking naar het huidige niveau van ongeveer 70.000. Dit geeft een bevolkings- dichtheid van net 308 personen per vierkante mijl (122 per vierkante km.) en daar ongeveer 40% van het eiland onbewoond is, is er altijd genoeg bewegingsruimte. Het belangrijkste bevolkingscentrum is Douglas, de hoofdstad, met circa 22.000 inwoners, terwijl er nog 28.000 wonen in zeven andere grotere steden en dorpen.

In dit groene, aangename en zeer vruchtbare land liggen veel verassingen! Het eiland heeft het oudste onafgebroken parlement ter wereld, zijn eigen muntstelsel, postzegels, telecommunicaties, taal, kastelen, legendes en douane, en dit alles samen met nog veel meer maken het eiland Man... "Engeland's best bewaarde eiland". Kom zelf maar kijken.

WILKOMMEN
DIE INSEL MAN – DIE BELIEBTE INSEL GROSSBRITANNIENS – WIR STELLEN VOR:

Seit Urzeiten bot die Insel Man ihren Besuchern einen flüchtigen Eindruck von allem, was in der Vergangenheit gut war – verbunden mit Erwartungen dafür, was die Zukunft bringen würde. Obgleich sie klein ist, hat sie es stets verstanden, ihre Schönheit und Köstlichkeiten in das rechte Licht zu rücken und sich in einer Weise mitzuteilen, daß sie jeden Winkel der Welt erreichte.

Geographisch liegt die Insel Man in der Mitte zwischen der englischen, irischen, schottischen und walisischen Küste – "den Nachbarinseln". Die Insel mißt an den äußersten Punkten 52 km mal 22 km und hat eine Landmasse von etwa 572 km². Sie bietet die verschiedensten Landschaftsbilder, wie sie an anderen Stellen auf den britischen Inseln zu finden sind, von offenen Hochmoorflächen, dicht bewaldeten Tälern bis zu mit Palmen umringten Teichen. Von über 160 km Küste umgeben, verläuft in nordöstlicher/südwestlicher Richtung in der Inselmitte ein Gebirgszug mit gut ausgebildeten Tälern, die in felsigen Klippen und geschützten Buchen enden. Dies steht im Kontrast zu den träge fließenden Bächen und Flüssen der flachen nördlichen Ebenen, die sich zu langen, sandigen Stränden schlängeln.

Auf der Insel Man herrscht ein ausgeglichenes Klima ohne Extreme, bedingt durch ihre Lage und den Einfluß des warmen Golfstromes, der ihre Küste umspielt. Der Wind weht meist von Südwesten. Dabei ist die ganze Insel durch ihre zerklüftete Topographie unterschiedlich geschützt oder dem Wind ausgesetzt. Nach Ende des Winters erweist sich das bessere Wetter im März und April für Besucher immer attraktiver. Im Sommer sind die Monate Mai und Juni gewöhnlich am trockensten, während Mai, Juni und Juli am sonnigsten sind. Juli und August sind am wärmsten, und in den meisten Fällen herrscht im September und Oktober schönes Wetter.

In den letzten Jahren nahm die Bevölkerung auf den derzeitigen Stand von etwa 70.000 zu. Damit entsteht eine Bevölkerungsdichte von ganzen 257 Einwohnern pro Quadratkilometer, und da etwa 40% der Insel unbewohnt sind, bietet sie immer genug Bewegungsfreiheit. Douglas, die Hauptstadt, hat die meisten Einwohner, etwa 22.000. Weitere 28.000 wohnen in sieben anderen größeren Städten und Dörfern.

Das grüne, angenehme und sehr fruchtbare Land bietet viele Überraschungen! Die Insel kann sich des ältesten fortgesetzten Parlaments der Welt rühmen, einer eigenen Währung, eigenen Sprache, Briefmarken, eines eigenen Fernmeldewesens, Schlössern, Legenden und Gebräuchen, und durch alles zusammen und vieles andere wird die Insel Man zur "beliebten Insel Großbritanniens". Besuchen Sie uns. Überzeugen Sie sich selbst.

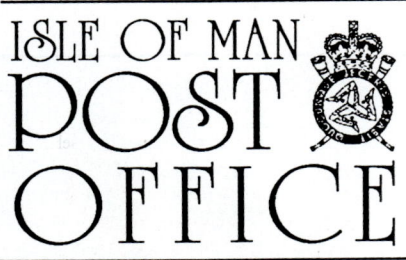

ISLE OF MAN POST OFFICE

Philatelic Bureau
P.O.Box 10.M
Douglas
Isle of Man
IM99 1PB
Tel.(0624) 686130

The 1993 Year Collection

Priced at only £17.00 This quality item makes an ideal Christmas gift. It contains all the Isle of Man Stamp Issues for 1993 and is packed with interesting background narrative. 24 illustrated pages in full colour. Bring to life your Isle of Man collection of more than 40 stamps on topics of worldwide interest with Manx connections.

Nigel Mansell (issued 1992) * Ship Definitives * Manx Electric Railway
Europa 1993 * Motorcycling Events * Butterflies * Christmas 1993

Please send me _____ 1993 Yearbook(s) @ £17.00 each incl. P & P
I enclose my remittance (Credit Card/Cheque/Postal Order) for £_____

Please debit my Access/Visa card No. ☐☐☐☐☐☐☐☐☐☐☐☐☐☐☐☐ Exp. Date __/__

Name_____

Address_____

(Please send your order to the address above)

8 Isle of Man

ONE MAN'S MAN

Snaefell Mountain Railway

JOHN HENDY

Step off the ferry at Douglas and within minutes you will be transported back into a bygone age. The Isle of Man lies in a time warp surrounded by the Irish Sea. It offers life as we imagine it was on the mainland many years ago with its cheery guest houses lining the promenade, the friendly clip-clop of the horse trams, the thousands of sparkling lights and people out to enjoy themselves in a well-ordered and timeless manner. They were happier, simpler, less stressful days when people were easier to please and were satisfied with what they had. A week on the Isle of Man was an annual event and was ample compensation for fifty one week's hard graft.

The horse trams are a reminder of an even older era and date from 1876. A leisurely trot from the Jubilee Clock along the Promenade to Derby Castle will bring the visitor to the southern terminus of the Manx Electric Railway which, as the Douglas and Laxey Coast Electric Tramway, celebrated its centenary in 1993. The original two trams, the oldest tramcars in the world still in use, may transport you across their switchback route to Ramsey, the Island's second town, via the delightful and picturesque village of Laxey. There you will find the only mixed gauge railway junction in the British Isles from where you can join the Snaefell Mountain Railway.

The four mile climb to the summit of the Island's highest point is a must for all visitors. The slow and gradual ascent along the side of Laxey Glen allows views of the famous Laxey Wheel, now restored and a reminder that in years gone by Laxey was a centre for lead and zinc mining. Workers from Cornwall moved in and the Lady Isabella wheel was constructed in 1854 to pump as much as 270 gallons of water a minute from mines which were as deep as Snaefell is high. They closed in 1929 and the area was cleared of its spoil heaps. Fortunately Lady Isabella survives to dominate her valley.

After crossing the T.T. Course, the tramroad entwines the summit of Snaefell (2,036 feet) before shuddering to a halt adjacent to the most welcome cafe. A short walk brings one to the top of the mountain which is marked by a small concrete obelisk known to the Ordnance Survey (who built it) as a triangulation pillar. As mountain tops go, it is not a particularly inspiring summit but, on a clear day, the view is unequalled within the British Isles.

To the east there rises the dark mass of the English Lake District, to the north are the rolling hills of Galloway in Scotland, to the west lie Ulster's Mountains of Mourne, to the south west are the Wicklow Mountains in the Republic of Ireland while to the south is Snowdonia in Wales. Five countries seen from one small island set aside from them all in the Irish Sea.

After witnessing such a supreme vista, the descent from the mountain can be something of an anticlimax and in no time the Snaefell tramcar will be sliding past the rows of grey miners' cottages back into Laxey from where many retrace their steps to Douglas through Fairy Cottage, Ballabeg, Baldrine, Groudle Glen and Onchan. Others continue via Cornaa, Ballajora and Dreemskerry to Ramsey, its sandy beaches sheltered beneath North Barrule, its harbour a favourite haven for scores of yachtsman.

Tucked away along by Douglas' inner harbour is a rather imposing red brick building which is the gateway to another of the island's unique institutions – the Isle of Man Steam Railway. Here one can be transported in a rickety coach behind a 120 year old railway locomotive to the picturesque south of the island along 16 miles of undulating track past elegant Castletown (the old capital of the Isle of Man) and pretty Port St. Mary to the centre of Port Erin, tucked away in the Island's south west corner. If time does not allow the visitor to explore, the railway museum is certainly worth a visit as is a cup of tea in the delightful station cafe. A close study of the memorabilia in the station waiting room is certainly recommended. Happy days!

The Port Erin line is all that remains of a once extensive railway system which also took the traveller through the Island's central valley to the ancient city of Peel where St. German's cathedral lies a ruin on St. Patrick's Isle. Two-thirds of the way through the valley between Douglas and Peel is St. John's – the historic centre of the Island where on Tynwald Day, 5th July, the Manx meet in an annual ceremony which has its origins with the Vikings. In the presence of the island's Lieutenant Governor and the Lord Bishop, upon the ancient Tynwald Hill they gather to hear in English and in Manx the laws and legislation passed in the preceding twelve months.

The Isle of Man is indeed a land apart with its own Parliament (Tynwald), laws and money. Until 1266 it was owned by Norway and was a separate country with its own King who also owned the Sodor, the southern isles of Scotland. Edward III was its first English king but in 1405, Henry IV gave it to the Stanley family and it later passed to the Dukes of Atholl. It was not until 1765 that it was sold to the British Government for £70,000. Today the Isle of Man is an independent member of the British Commonwealth.

From St. John's, another railway line cut southwards towards the Foxdale lead mines which were dug beneath the shadow of nearby South Barrule. A further railway line ran the easy way up the west coast of the island through Kirk Michael and approached the east coast and Ramsey along the northern edge of the upland, through Ballaugh and Sulby.

The Island's unique transport system is for many its greatest charm but the trams and engines have not been assembled specifically to pull in the tourists. Quite the reverse in fact – these are the originals! They have not been replaced simply because the money was never available and they survived until such time when it was realised that these simple modes of transportation, these relics of Victorian Britain, remained when all others had been swept away in the name of the all conquering 'progress.' Sample the Island's transport system and anyone young or old, with an ounce of feeling for the past, will immediately be captivated. To many visitors, the Island provides an escape from the twentieth century.

But it is not only the human input which makes the Island special but the nature and scale of the land itself. There is something in its Celtishness and in its Norseness which sets it apart from the rest of Britain. It is Cornwall and Ulster, Scotland and Wales all rolled into one. The rugged and wild centre of the Island, its mountains and moorland, are best explored on foot and it is easy to travel off the beaten track and away from the crowds. Large boulders, deposited by glaciers during the last ice advance, litter much of the upland areas and heather, ling, fern and gorse are in profusion. Lower down there are quiet, sheltered

Lady of Mann

lanes lined by foxgloves and wild fuschia. The occasional bleat of a sheep or the song of a bird are the only sounds while the salt-laiden sea breezes set the tall grasses in continuous motion. Within the Manx hedgerows it is possible to see wild flowers which, due to the gross over use of weedkillers and pesticides, have disappeared from other parts of Britain. Its rich variety of landscape presents the island as Britain in miniature – from the steep wave-lashed cliffs of the south to the flat plains of Ayre in the north.

The Island is also rich in history with Norse stone circles and long houses, signs of early Christianity and plenty of evidence of man's first struggles to farm the land. The ancient Manx Celtic language seems to be undergoing something of a revival and will be noticed in use on road name signs. Place names too give an indication as to the settlement's history e.g. places ending in by, as in Sulby and Jurby are Scandinavian for 'farm' and Snaefell means, the 'snow mountain.'

The gateway to the Isle of Man is, of course, Douglas and the best place from which to see the Island's capital is from high up on Douglas Head. There the whole of Douglas Bay as far as Onchan Head is spread out before you with its endless procession of hotels and guest houses lining the front and backed by the mass of Snaefell. Close-by the onlooker and to the left, the rivers Dhoo and Glass (which came to give the present town its name) empty into the harbour. At its Victoria and Edward Piers thousands of Manx have sailed away to seek fame and fortune while others departed by steamer to fight for King and country. During both World Wars, the Island was used as a huge internment camp and between times, millions of holiday makers have arrived in the elegant vessels of the Isle of Man Steam Packet Company.

Founded in 1830, the company is still fiercely independent and during the summer months offers no fewer than five destinations. In days gone by the Steam Packet owned and operated up to a dozen ships most of which would be brought out of mothballs simply for the summer period when the Island's tourist industry was at its zenith. Each of the Lancashire mill towns would have its wakes week

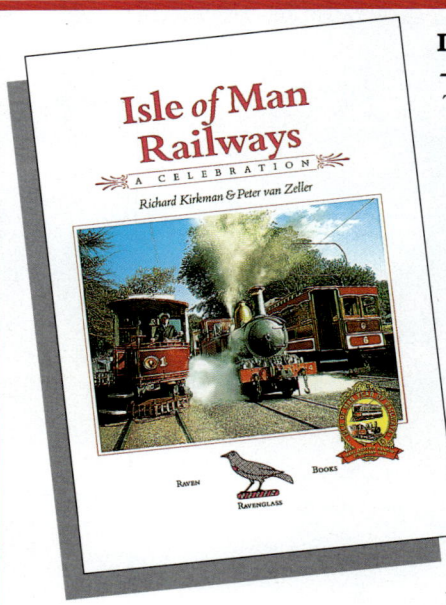

ISLE OF MAN RAILWAYS – A CELEBRATION

The Isle of Man is a narrow gauge railway paradise where considerable parts of an elaborate network still exist. Horse, steam and electric powered services still operate with original Victorian rolling stock along some of the most scenic routes in the British Isles.

The book celebrates 100 years of the Manx Electric Railway and provides a comprehensive survey of the entire Island system - past and present . Profusely illustrated with over 100 photographs and 34 maps, this 96 page hardback book is available from booksellers and on Isle of Man Steam Packet ships for just £8.95. *The ideal holiday souvenir!*

Raven Books, Ravenglass,Cumbria.

Discover Britain's Treasured Island

Come to an island with a thousand years of history and a million things to explore. From beautiful broad beaches to tiny hidden coves. From breathtaking scenery to mouthwatering cuisine.
This year you can explore a host of great offers too, including considerable savings if you book early and a chance to win a holiday.
Send off now for your free copy of the latest Holiday Guide.

HOLIDAY PRICE GUIDE
5 nights B&B by air from
£143
per person
(Inc. Saturday night)
Car Hire from £87

Once you arrive we can help you plan your holiday. Our Tourist Information Bureau are to be found in all the main tourist areas, with helpful staff ready to let you know what's on and where to visit, with ideas for the whole family.

Welcome to the Smile of Man.

FREE 112-page Holiday Guide

Please fill in the coupon or call 0345 686868 (local call rates apply) for your free copy of the latest Official Isle of Man Holiday Guide.

Name ....

Address ....

....

.... Postcode ....

Would you like more information
sent to you later in the year?   Yes ❑   No ❑

Please send to Department of Tourism, Sea Terminal, Douglas, Isle of Man, IM1 2RG.

and literally close down while its occupants filled the steamers for Douglas. They came in their hundreds of thousands to breathe the fresh air, to 'get away from it all' and to see for themselves the island's natural beauty. The Island groaned and creaked with its tourists, the guest houses were packed and tented villages even sprang up to accommodate the thousands of young men who preferred the healthier and cheaper option. It was the Steam Packet, coupled with the growth of railway communication on the British mainland, which made the Manx tourist industry and turned Douglas from a small fishing village into a flourishing resort.

At one time some half a million people visited the Island each year and amongst the busiest times were in early June during the period of the famous Isle of Man Tourist Trophy Races. The original races, started by the RAC in 1904, were for motor cars but three years later motor cycles were introduced. Today, the T.T. races attract thousands of leather-clad enthusiasts from all over the world and at this time the course roads are closed to all but the brave competitors who pit their wits against the steep banks, stone walls and tight turns in the toughest of all tests.

At the end of the season, the Steam Packet's fleet returned one by one to their winter quarters and the islanders were left to themselves for the winter months. Inevitably, with the decline in the Island's holiday trade, this state of affairs has dramatically changed and today the two ships of the Steam Packet carry just as many islanders as holiday makers. Traditional seaside holidays have become a thing of the past. Cheap 'all-in' packages to the Costa del Something-or-other, guarantee sunshine and warmth and the pleasure seeking, fun-loving, types have turned their backs on the bucket and spade holiday. When it were rainin', there were nowt to do.

Beyond the Victoria Pier is the Tower of Refuge which was constructed one hundred and fifty years ago so that shipwrecked sailors could shelter from the gales and storms that had driven their vessels onto the notorious Conister Rock. The Douglas which faces the sea today was the work of Governor Loch during the late Victorian period. Under his jurisdiction, the promenade was built protecting the town from the sea and rows of boarding houses

Point of Ayre Lighthouse

sprang up between the existing buildings. As a result of the increase in tourists, in order to entertain them there followed the construction of places of fun and amusement. The Palace, with its dance floor of sixteen thousand square feet and space for five thousand people, was built in the 1890s and the wonderful and untouched Gaiety Theatre of 1900 stands today as a loving testimony to that era.

The Isle of Man is some 32 miles long and 12 miles wide. During my visits I have experienced for myself that great sense of nostalgia which I hope this short piece will have captured. I have seen enough of the Island to give me a simple flavour and understanding of the place and the desire to return to explore further but only a very old and wise visitor would claim that he actually *knows* the Isle of Man. A part of its charm and mystery lies in the fact that no matter how many times one steps ashore at Douglas, there is still more to see and learn.

The Island has something for everyone. It is a land of contrasts and although its isolation can certainly be a source of frustration to those wishing to visit it more often, it is this very isolation that has preserved both its peerless character and its unique atmosphere.

John Hendy

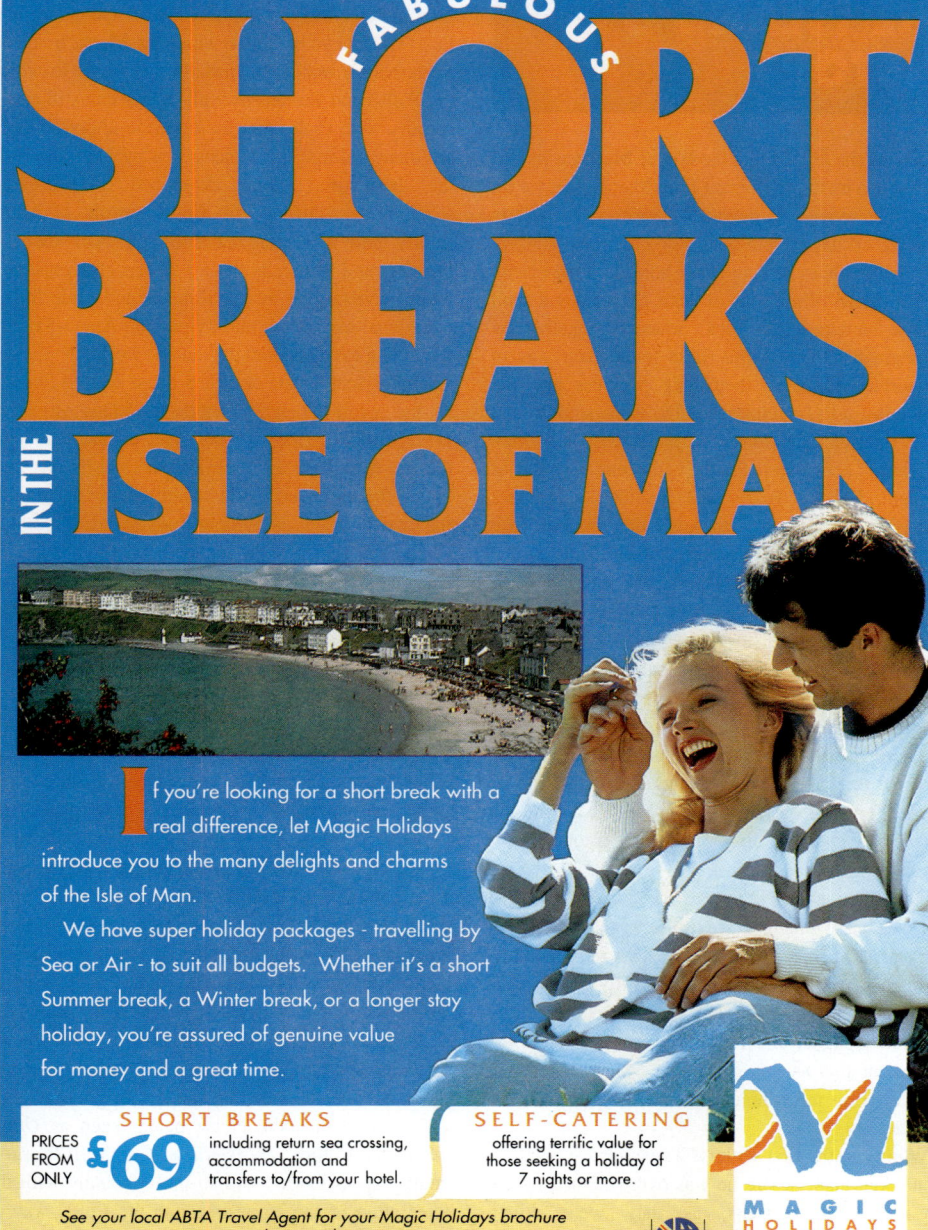

THE ISLAND'S HISTORY

Despite the legend that the Isle of Man was hurled into the sea by the Irish giant Finn Mac Coole, we do know that something moved in those crystal waters in the far off days of pre-history.

Something was stirring at the bottom of the ocean. Over a period of millions of years the mud and sand became hardened into rock. Squeezed together by unimaginable forces these rocks found their way to the surface to begin their long progress into the mountains, hills, precipitous cliffs, valleys, glens and plains that we know today. At times the Isle of Man has been connected to the adjacent islands of England, Ireland, Wales and Scotland... at other times not. Occasionally these hidden forces broke forth pouring lava and ash out onto the land, as can still be witnessed between Scarlett Point and Poyll Vaaish. The sea has always remained pre-eminent in the Island's life and history.

Thousands of years ago, ancient Mann protruded above the ice in the shape of three islands, a form now scarcely recognisable, save for the high lands of the North, South and the Mull Peninsula. As the ice retreated the harsh landscape was sculptured into its present form. In its farewell, the ice left behind the gift of the lovely rolling Bride hills, formed from glacial deposits.

Now lying quietly in the Irish Sea, the Isle of Man has seen many changes in both physical and human terms as it emerged from its formation into the dawn of history itself. It now seems hardly credible as modern man gazes down into the central valley between Douglas and Peel, that this was once the seabed, or that as you drive between Port St Mary and Port Erin this whole area was covered in water and ice.

Who were the first settlers? The evidence points to Stone Age man, before he was overwhelmed by the physically larger Celts, as they were driven westwards by the all conquering Germans and Romans.

Settling into a very pleasant and fertile land suited the new immigrants who belonged to a separate and very distinct tribe from the Celts to the South and East. The Gaelic branch to which the Manx, Irish and Scots belong and the Cymric or Brythonic to which the Welsh and Bretons owe allegiance can still easily identify with each other by language although there are many cultural differences. It is probably towards the Irish that there developed the greatest similarities... and so the Celtic people of Mann settled into a routine of common land owning, farming and generally living a peaceful existence totally undisturbed by the Romans and, save for an occasional marauding raid by passing Anglo-Saxons, remaining isolated from the outside world.

This peaceful state of affairs could not last forever. By the end of the eighth century the Island was about to receive its first visitors. No ordinary tourists these... they were the Vikings, who had by this time begun their wanderings in search of plunder around the British islands, western and southern Europe.

The sea held no fear for these brave and warlike warriors who believed that plundering was an honourable occupation. The long sandy and sometimes gravelly beaches of the North and West of the Island proved more than suitable for their longboats to be run ashore and there was shelter aplenty to the South and East. Fifty years or so after their first arrival, they began to settle down to a life ashore and this is evident in the names of some of our farms, mountains, hills, villages and people to this very day.

The Norse settlers in their language used *by* as the ending to many of their words and so you have *Kirby* meaning Church farm, *Colby* meaning Kolli's farm, *Jurby* as Ivar's farm, and there are many other words of Scandinavian extract. For example *Snaefell* means Snow Mountain, *Sartfell* is Black Hill. Sulby still exists as a village, in those far off days it was known as Solvi. On the lips of a Gaelic speaking people these new words took on a different pronunciation and so you have the Norse names such as *Ottarr* becoming Cottier, *Thorketill* as Corkhill, *Thorliotr* ending up as Corlett and so on. Gradually with the integration of the Norsemen into the Celtic way of life many of our commonest surnames began to emerge such as Brew, Bridson, Cain, Caley, Callister, Callow, Cannell, Cashen, Clucas, Curphey,

A Deemster (Manx High Court Judge) taking part in the annual Tynwald Ceremony

Viking long boat – Peel

Cowin, Kaighan, Kelly, Kewley, Mylchreest, Mylrea, Quayle, Quiggin and Quinney as well as many others.

With the coming together of the two races, the Island began a further period of turbulent development. Tradition tells of the arrival of the first Norse King of Man, *Goree* or Orry as we now know him, at the Lhane in Jurby who, when asked where he came from, responded by pointing at the Milky Way and said "that is the road to my country". The Manx thereafter knew the Milky Way as *Yn raad mooar Ree Goree,* "the great road of King Orry".

During the period the Isle of Man was under Viking control it was ruled at various times by kings who sometimes lived in Dublin, Northumbria or in Mann itself. After a short period in the hands of the Norse rulers of Limerick towards the end of the tenth century, it became subject to the rule of the Earls of Orkney before falling into the hands of the Kings of Dublin once again.

In 1079, Godred Crovan, son of Harald the Black of Iceland, came to conquer Mann. After being defeated by the Manx in his first two battles against them, he returned and in his third attack was successful, largely because he hid three hundred of his followers amongst the trees on Sky Hill above Milntown. Because he had been well received by the Manx on fleeing to the Isle of Man after the defeat of Harald, King of Norway, at the battle of Stamford Bridge in 1066, he spared the defeated Manx. After the battle he contented himself with dividing the Island in two, with the Manx retaining the northern half and the Vikings living in the southern half. Godred's descendants were to rule Mann for nearly two hundred years.

During the transition period from warriors of the seas to landowners and farmers, the Vikings left the Celts, who for a while were little more than slaves, to run the farms and harvest the crops. The Norsemen busied themselves trading with the adjacent islands, Iceland and the South of Europe. Probably their best known occupation on land was to carve beautiful crosses, many fine examples of which still exist today dotted about in our churchyards and museums.

Without doubt the greatest single gift the Vikings donated to the Isle of Man was the system of government which still exists today. The historian will tell you that Tynwalds or *Things* as the Vikings called them were probably held in each sheading. These smaller *Things* came together at least once a year under the auspices of a great *Thing* for the whole Island. After more than one thousand years of continuous parliamentary government, the Island still remains well placed in the forefront of democracy, and the modern Manx Nation continues to export and trade its products to the rest of the world much as their Viking forefathers did many centuries ago.

Although the Vikings eventually became Christians, it was not before they had extinguished the light of Christianity which had burned brightly on Mann from about the fourth century onwards. Around the beginning of the eleventh century the Manx began once again to embrace Christianity. Although written evidence is scanty, from the time of the founding of Rushen Abbey by the Cistercians of Furness Abbey in Barrow, it is possible to get a clearer picture of developments from the writings of the monks.

The Manx bishops are known as the Bishops of Sodor and Man, and the earliest reference to the Diocese of Sodor and Man seems to be in 1154. Consisting of the southern islands of Scotland, it extended from the Hebrides to Arran and the Isle of

Man itself. Sodor owes its derivation from two Norse words meaning southern isles, so in fact Sodor and Man means "The southern Isles and Man".

Bishops have always played an important role in the history of this fair land, sometimes leading the people by good example, at other times abusing their power and privileged position. In 1266 the connection between the "Isles and Sodor" came to an end, although the diocese continued to be under the rule of a distant Norwegian Archbishop until the fifteenth century. During this period the Island had been divided into parishes.

After Norse rule had come to an end, the Isle of Man was the subject of many struggles which saw its ownership passing between the Scots and the English. It was not until 1346 that the Island came firmly and finally under English rule. During this period immediately before the long reign of the Stanleys, the Island's people suffered grievously. Contemporary writings of the time report that the Island was "desolate and full of wretchedness". In another report the writer told of a great battle on the slopes of South Barrule in which the Manx were heavily defeated by Irish freebooters who plundered everything of value. Only the purchase of corn from Ireland saved the people from starvation. So poor were the islanders that they could no longer afford to make any more of the magnificent crosses for which they had been renowned in earlier times.

The Stanley dynasty which was to rule the Isle of Man from 1405 – 1736 presented their first King of Man as Sir John Stanley I. He never came to the Island and was succeeded by his son Sir John Stanley II a wise but somewhat despotic ruler, who at least conferred some benefits on the people. It is recorded that there were two revolts against his authority. To prevent a repetition he increased the power of the governors, and at this period he substituted trial by battle with trial by jury as a means of settling disputes. Many of his successors did not visit their kingdom, and those who did come, often only paid a fleeting visit.

History records that we had to wait for James Stanley, the 7th Earl of Derby, for the next major turning point in the story of Mann. In 1643 James, or as the Manx people called him, *Yn Stanlagh Mooar*, The Great Stanley, was ordered by King Charles I of

View from Tynwald Hill

England to go to the Isle of Man and put down a threatened revolt by the Manx. Hiding an iron hand in a velvet glove he soon made himself popular. Although the people of this period enjoyed peace never had they had less liberty. In fact they were actually deprived of their ancient tenure or, in other words, the right to hold land.

With Charles II on the throne of England, *Yn Stanlagh Mooar* threw in his lot once more with the Royalists. Leading his troops, three hundred Manxmen amongst them, he set off in support of the King. Disaster overtook those brave men and Stanley himself was executed. At this time the great Manx patriot William Christian, *Illiam Dhone* appeared... to save the people from disaster. *Illiam Dhone,* which translated into English means "Brown William", anticipated punitive action against the Islanders and gathered together the people at Ronaldsway to assess the future. Dispatching the militia to capture all military installations he achieved total success, with the exception of Peel and Rushen castles, which were soon given up by Stanley's widow, and the Island eventually surrendered to the Parliamentarians.

William Christian paid a terrible price for his actions. After the Restoration and some ten years

Cregneash

after leading the revolt against the Countess of Derby, *Illiam Dhone* was shot to death on Hango Hill at Castletown.

The 1700's were turbulent years for the Manx Nation. They saw the end of the Stanleys' rule, serious disputes with the English Parliament, and the destruction of the smuggling trade which was just about the only way the Island had been financially "kept afloat". On the credit side it saw the passing of The Act of Settlement in 1704, which is effectively the Island's Magna Carta, and in 1736 under the rule of the 2nd Duke of Atholl, the Manx Bill of Rights was introduced. This Bill in effect did away with despotic government and replaced it with oligarchical government or, in other words, the Keys – the lower house of Tynwald – once more reverted to self election. Constitutional Government was just around the corner.

Working hard for the people over half a century during this era was the much loved Bishop Thomas Wilson. Bishop of Sodor and Man for fifty eight years, he fed the populace in times of crop failure, promoted education, established schools and libraries around the Island, and laboured long on behalf of the Manx State.

On the 11th July 1765 the Island passed into the ownership of the British Crown. As the Manx standard was lowered at Castle Rushen and the Union flag raised, George III was proclaimed King of Man… John the 3rd Duke of Atholl had sold the Island to the Imperial Parliament for £70,000. The prosperity of the Island, such as it was, disappeared overnight with the demise of the smuggling trade and London appeared well satisfied. This was not to be the end of the Atholl connections with the Isle of Man.

As the Island fell into decay and its people into despair, the Government in London felt obliged to try and rectify this parlous state of affairs and in 1793 appointed the 4th Duke to be Governor. This appointment was not a success and in 1829 he severed his relationship with the Island for the sum of £417,000 and left. George IV, King of Great Britain and Ireland became Lord of Man.

The period immediately after the Dukes' departure saw little change. London continued to control the Island's revenue, and the House of Keys still largely ignored the peoples' wishes by electing one of their "own" whenever a vacancy in the House occurred. Help was at hand though in the form of Mr. Henry Loch, later to be Lord Loch and after whom part of Douglas Promenade is named.

Appointed as Governor in 1863, Henry Loch brought energy and a real sense of purpose to the position. Working closely with Tynwald Court, lengthy negotiations with Her Britannic Majesty's Government were eventually concluded in 1866 to ensure that after the running expenses of the Manx Government were met, any surpluses could be retained on the Isle of Man for improvements to a fledgling infrastructure. Part of the agreement called for the House of Keys to be popularly elected and for the English Government to receive a sum of £10,000 annually from insular revenue as a contribution towards the defence of the Realm, a payment that, although much increased, continues to this very day.

Even before the arrival of Governor Loch, the Island had started to become popular as a tourist destination. Certainly with more and more of the revenue being retained locally and spent on improving the infrastructure, it was not too long before the population increased and communications to and from the Island vastly improved.

Towards the end of the 1800's as the railways and their associated shipping companies opened up the adjacent islands to travel for all, tourism in the Isle of Man mushroomed. Much of the infrastructure that exists today owes its initial development to this period. Hotels, trains, piers, theatres, reservoirs, steamships and roads all played their part in thrusting the Island to the forefront of the domestic British leisure market.

As the new post Victorian era arrived, the Island rose to the challenge of mass tourism and for decades happily served the Lancashire cotton workers, the Yorkshire miners, Scottish engineers, Geordie ship builders and a whole host of other folk and their families as they sought their annual escape from a life of hard work on the fair shores of Ellan Vannin. A tradition that was only interrupted by two world wars.

During the twentieth century the Isle of Man, like many other places around the world, has witnessed change to its economy. As the old and traditional industries declined, new methods of sustaining the population arose. As our motto says, *Quocunque Jeceris Stabit...* Which Ever Way You Throw Me I Will Stand. Investment in tourism continues apace. What has never changed though, is the traditional Manx welcome offered to our visitors.

Please enjoy our Island as much as we enjoy your visiting us.

Hango Hill, Castletown

What's happening on the Isle of Man TODAY?

Its all in *the manx post*

The Visitors Guide to All Events

All the latest information about events, attractions, places to eat, the Victorian railways, the Story of Mann & Manx Museum sites, souvenirs, children's activities, entertainment, folklore, walks, car hire, sport and golf in a colourful tabloid newspaper.

Available from Newsagents & on the Ferries too!

COASTS AND ISLANDS

COASTS

Mythological legend informs us that the Isle of Man came into being as the result of an argument between two warriors, one in Ireland, Finn MacCoole, and one of unknown name in the adjacent island of England. During the course of their dispute a large lump of Ireland was hurled from the vicinity of Lough Neagh and missing its intended target landed in the middle of the North Irish Sea... and that's how the Isle of Man arrived!

The sea has always played an integral part in the development of the Island and it is no surprise that the coastline still ranks importantly in our lives. Stand anywhere on the sea's edge and look at the views. To the East there rises the impressive bulk of the Cumbrian mountains and the English Lake District, to the North are the purple headed hills of Galloway in Scotland, over to the West lie Ulster's Mountains of Mourne, to the South West the Republic of Ireland's Wicklow Mountains loom above the horizon, while to the South is Snowdonia in Wales, clearly seen on a fine day. With five countries as neighbours, it is a wonder that this small Island has remained segregated from the hustle and bustle of modern life for so long.

The seemingly endless changing contours of the cliffs, crowded into such a small land mass leaves no room for boredom. Indeed it is difficult to imagine where else in the British Islands you could be offered such a wide variety of coastal scenery. From the steep wave-lashed cliffs of the East and South to the long sandy cliffs of the North and West there is choice for everyone.

From Douglas heading South, the cliffs gradually diminish in height all the way down to *Poyll Vaaish* to the West of Castletown. On past the low-lying shores of Bay ny Carrickey the cliffs from Port St Mary to the Sound seem suddenly to rear up from the deep waters surrounding the Mull Peninsula. The Manx National Trust area to the South of Cregneash

Derbyhaven

Village boasts some of the most dramatic cliff scenery on the Island. Tradition says that some great upheaval in the earth's crust aeons ago stacked up great blocks of rock to form the Chasms. Modern science indicates that a more likely explanation is that their incredible shape was formed by the action of wind and waves down through the centuries. Warning, there are deep holes in the Chasms often hidden beneath your feet by clumps of springy heather. Please take care and keep tight control of any children in your party. Spanish Head is a promontory associated with the Spanish Armada. Folklore informs us that a galleon was wrecked here as the English navy chased the survivors of that great event down through the Irish Sea. It would be doubtful if anyone got ashore from such an incident.

The cliffs from the Sound to Port Erin are as rugged as those on the East side of the peninsula. The sheer drops into the sea leave no room for complacency and great care must be exercised when walking in this area. If you are crossing the edge of Bay Fine, look down – you may be lucky and see Basking sharks close in on the coast, sometimes it helps to wear a pair of sunglasses to see them.

Perched spectacularly on Port Erin's Bradda Head is Milner's Tower. The tower can be reached by following the pretty coastal footpath from Bradda Glen or by driving part of the way up a minor road from Bradda West. Although the permanent

coastguard look-out post is no longer, the Isle of Man's own Coastguard Service do keep watch from the Head in certain bad weather conditions. The views from the top of the tower are second to none and there is a plaque indicating the position from which a world prize-winning photograph was taken in 1936. Built in 1871 as a memorial to William Milner, the head of a firm of Liverpool safe manufacturers, it is built in the shape of the barrel of a lock, with the inner end uppermost.

Port Erin to *Gob yn Ushtey* (Point of Water or Waterfall) has the highest cliffs on the Isle of Man rising in places over a thousand feet out of the water. The cliffs here act as a huge windbreak, affording protection from the strong westerlys, to the farms to the East. *Cronk ny Arrey Laa* dwarfs even the grandeur of Spanish Head as it tumbles precipitously 1,500 feet to the sea. Stretching away northwards the cliffs dip down to Niarbyl and then gradually rise up, past and beyond Glen Maye, peaking at Contrary Head, before plunging down almost to sea level at Peel Castle. Interestingly Contrary Head, it is said, was named from the fact that the SE-going and NW-going tidal streams divide and meet off this headland.

Peel like Port Erin has its own tower looking down on it from a height. Standing on the summit of Corrin's Hill, it is believed that the remains of a Quaker and his family are buried here. A few yards from Corrin's Tower is a sacred place, much revered by the early Christians, St Patrick's Well. Tradition has it that when St Patrick landed there, the silver-shod horse he was riding shed a shoe and on that very spot a spring of water gushed from the rock and formed a well. The pathway to Corrin's Memorial gently threads its way through the lush green turf and when in season, the heather, bracken and gorse that does so much to brighten the hillside. From the Stack, the Point to the North end of Peel Bay, the coastline changes from sandstone cliffs to high sandy headlands. Mother nature has been busy here and in severe weather large sections of the coast have been washed away. Kirk Michael to Blue Point is a coast of moderately high sandy cliffs but very much changed to fine sanded dunes. The Ayres really have no cliffs. The sea laps the very edge of the flat plains and it is not until Cranstal is reached that any height is gained by the coast.

With sandy cliffs bordering the northern end of Ramsey Bay the coastline of Mann suddenly breaks back into ruggedness, with the massive headland of Maughold looming out of the crystal clear waters beyond Ramsey's southern flank. Rounding the vertical walls of Maughold Head and its fine lighthouse, the cliffs plunge down to Port Mooar and then rise ever upwards until their high point, in the vicinity of Dhoon Bay. Laxey is tucked into the mouth of the Great Glen, protected by Laxey Head to the North and from the southerly winds by the bulk of Clay Head.

On past Clay Head, an example of the anglicisation of the Manx language but admittedly so much easier to pronounce than *Kione ny Cleigh*, lies *Groudle*. This part of the parish of Onchan owes its origins to the Scandinavian word Krappdalr, Narrow Glen. At the North end of Douglas Bay lies Port Jack. Tradition has it that it got its name from the mate of a small ship feeling its way South along the coast in foggy weather. Perhaps it was the sound of the breakers on the shore that made him call out "Port Jack, Port Jack" and the Captain duly obliged and headed out to sea again.

ISLANDS

The Isle of Man has only one real satellite island although there are a number of small islets. Being an island race we are very possessive of our country and anything that rises even a few feet above sea level is claimed and if possible nominated for island status. The main island is the Calf of Man. In the ownership of the Manx National Trust it is possible to visit the Calf during the summer months. If you don't have your own boat, regular sailings operate from Port Erin and occasionally from Port St Mary. Should you be using your own boat, take care, the waters surrounding the Calf are dangerous and should be treated with the greatest of respect. Do not go too close to the shoreline, several drying rocks project from the base of the cliffs and the coast is foul to a distance of 2 cables (for the landlubbers that is about 185 metres or 608 feet) offshore. There are two harbours or to be more specific two landing places on the Calf. South Haven which is a small inlet close to the East of *The Burroo,* Dome-shaped Hill – the name of the nearby large rock – and Grants Harbour, little more than a cleft in the rocks on the North East corner.

The Calf has a circumference of five miles and a land mass of about 1,000 acres and is now a is a bird sanctuary of international repute. There is a long history to the Island but it seems as if it never had a large population, a legacy perhaps of the strong currents that flow around its shores and the difficult landing conditions. A Celtic stone cross of great antiquarian value was discovered there many years ago which is believed to have been from a long since lost ancient keeill. In the dangerous years of the English Civil War, *Yn Stanlagh Mooar* fortified the Calf, for a rental to the owner of 500 puffins a year. The only crofting now done on the Calf is sheep farming and there is a fine flock of Loaghtan sheep roaming freely about the Island.

The cliffs and wide expanses of springy turf and heather are nesting grounds to a colossal variety of bird life and the Island is well populated by rabbits. Walking can be hazardous with thousands of rabbit holes penetrating the ground. Brer Rabbit must have been the main source of food there, for a story is told about an inhabitant who not only used them for food but also as payment for his rent, and who became so fed up with his diet that he composed a prayer known as the "Calf of Man Grace".

> For rabbits hot, and rabbits cold,
> For rabbits young, and rabbits old,
> For rabbits tender, rabbits tough,
> I thank the Lord, I've had enough.

Off the South West corner of the Calf is a small islet called the Chicken Rock. The rock is named from the once numerous Mother Carey's Chickens, a seabird which frequent the waters of the area. Standing sentinel over a dangerous reef is a tall granite lighthouse. Built in 1875 to replace two earlier lighthouses on the Calf, this guardian of shipping is now un-manned and fully automated as a consequence of a fire in 1964, from which the Keepers were lucky to escape with their lives.

The sea passage between the Calf of Man and the Isle of Man is divided into two channels by a small island called *Kitterland*. The derivation of this name is shrouded in the mists of the past. There is an argument that the name comes from the Scandinavian word the latter part of which means island, with the first part being either a personal name or Kid's (as in goat). Probably the more romantic and more acceptable definition of the name is from the great Baron Kitter who was wrecked there in the days of Olaf. In 1852 the brig "Lily" was wrecked on Kitterland and subsequently exploded killing all the salvors, save one. It ranks as one of the worst shipping disasters to befall the Isle of Man. There is a monument to the victims in Rushen churchyard.

The mariner sailing up the West coast searching for islands to shelter behind in stormy weather will be disappointed. Between Port Erin and Peel there is but one place which could even be remotely described as an island. Lying below Elby Point at Niarbyl is a rock which is much frequented by sea anglers and it is certain that little more than a coracle would find safety there. The disappointed mariner soon cheers up however when he reaches the fishing port of Peel.

Built around the estuary of the River Neb, Peel's outer boundaries are protected by the imposing Peel Castle, sitting astride St Patrick's Isle. Now no longer technically an island, St Patrick's Isle is joined to the Manx mainland by a causeway. Bridging Fenella's Beach, the causeway takes the visitor onto an island whose history is as fascinating as it is possibly unequalled by anywhere else in the known world. Within its five acres, almost every period of architecture from prehistoric earthworks to the fortifications erected during the Napoleonic wars is represented. It witnessed the early struggles of Christian missionaries against the Pagans. At various times down through the ages it has been a garrisons, an armoury and a place of retreat, in more troubled

Sarita (the Witch of the Sound) invites you to the unique SOUND CAFE
Daily Specials, Hot Meals
Home-made Soups, Quiche,
Cakes, Scones and Sandwiches
OPEN 7 DAYS A WEEK 10.30 am-5.30 pm

Niarbyl Bay

times. In the past it has been used as a ecclesiastical prison and there are believed to be no less than eight bishops buried there. As an interesting footnote, Bishop Wilson in 1725 was in dispute with Lieutenant-Governor Thomas Horton, over the latter's plan to remove the roof remains from the Island's St Germain's Cathedral and use them in the building of new stables in Castletown. It seems that the vessel used to carry away the Cathedral's roof timbers was lost on its subsequent voyage. A place to whet the appetite of anyone with even the slightest of interest in the past!

Coasting northwards round the Point of Ayre the mariner finds a shoreline devoid of islands until Douglas Bay is reached. Everyone who makes their landfall in Douglas cannot help but be impressed by the picturesque building that graces Conister or St Mary's Rock. Known as the Tower of Refuge, it was built by Sir William and Lady Hillary in 1832 as a refuge to shelter the shipwrecked sailors from vessels that had been driven by gales and storms onto these jagged and dangerous rocks. It acted as the spur to Sir William and he went on to become the founder of the Royal National Lifeboat Institution – the RNLI.

To complete the tour of Manxland's islands the journey will take you to St Michael's Island. Lying just off the North East point of the Langness Peninsula, it is joined to the mainland by a stone built causeway. Looking at the map it almost seems as if the promontory is boot shaped with St Michael's Island forming the heel. Often known as Fort Island... what historical events this small island must have witnessed. The island guards Derbyhaven from the worst excesses of East and South East gales and as such was well used by the Vikings and others to shelter their boats.

The remains of the only buildings standing on the island are of a round, stone built fort and a chapel. Built in the seventeenth century the fort is in very good condition and has a date, 1645 inscribed on a stone above the gateway. The Seventh Earl of Derby, *Yn Stanlagh Mooar* must have feared for his Kingdom to erect this fortification. Remains of earth embankments are still clearly visible on the Island and it is thought that they may have been raised at the time of Magnus's landing here in 1250. The ruined chapel probably stands on the site of an ancient keeill

Peel Castle

and a close inspection of the building reveals alterations at different times to its dimensions.

A local story tells of a much loved priest who was famous amongst the inhabitants for his teachings and kind heart, and who proposed that a new church should be built on St Michael's Isle. The idea of this twelfth or early thirteenth century church had come to him in a vision. In the vision, St Michael pointed out to the priest the location of the building and a finely designed altar within. Working with a will the people gave their labour freely and soon had finished the church. There was however no way that their meagre resources could provide the fine altar seen in the vision… that was, until the confession of a dying shipwrecked pirate revealed a horde of gold buried in the churchyard. At first hesitant to heed the dying pirate's encouragement to use it for the good of the people, the priest refused. Eventually convinced that there was no one left alive to whom the treasure could belong, this kindly man of God bought a statue of the Madonna and around its neck hung a string of pearls, found with the treasure trove.

One day a vessel came to an anchor in Derbyhaven and two of the crew came ashore, begging the priest to come out to their vessel and minister to one of their colleagues. Suspecting nothing, he went with them. Alas it was another pirate ship, a sister to the one from which the dying pirate had been saved; they had come in search of their treasure. The next morning the villagers found the church had been sacked and their priest murdered by the very pearls from the statue's neck. To this very day it is believed that whoever strikes the walls of this ancient building will hear the moans of the saintly victim, accompanied by the jingle of coins.

Point of Ayre

MOUNTAINS, VALLEYS, GLENS AND PARKS

Mountains in whatever country you are visiting have a mystique of their own. They draw your eyes ever skyward, almost enticing you to climb them.

What they also guarantee, especially in the northern hemisphere are large areas of unspoilt countryside. The Isle of Man is no exception to the rule with some 40% of its land mass un-inhabited. There are twenty five peaks over 1,000 feet in height and the many of them are well over 1,500 feet above sea level. The Manx mountains have a finely sculptured appearance almost as if they have been moulded by a giant artist. Snaefell has pride of place as Ellan Vannin's highest peak. You can never tire of looking at it from most places on the Island… and it is home to the finest mountain railway in the British Isles.

Once into the mountains there is a magic feel to the surroundings, almost an atmospheric tingle. No day in the mountains is the same as any other. The light plays on the slopes in an almost musical way. Here a dark patch, there bright light and always, the shadows of the clouds chasing across hillsides. All the seasons of the year have a beauty of their own in the mountains, in direct contrast to the previous or succeeding season. It is as if the peaks keep trying on new overcoats, sometimes green, at other times a multi-coloured quilted jacket. Slopes covered in heather and *ling*, the old Norse word for a heather type of plant – drifting down into bracken and gorse. The Good Lord's handiwork certainly gives great pleasure and a feeling of contentment in the Mountains of Mann.

The mountains have been guardians to the peace of the Island, serving as lookout posts in times of threat. Indeed careful perusal of the OS will show that there is more than one mountain or hill by the name of *Cronk ny Arrey Laa*, the Hill of the Day Watch.

VALLEYS

There are no great valleys on the Isle of Man, the size of the Island prevented that, but the two areas of mountains are divided by the central valley running in a South East/North West direction between Douglas and Peel. Approaching the Island by sea from England the first detail seen on the landfall is the Fall of Greeba, a purple, tree clad slope that always tells Manx homecomers they are back! Greeba lies about half-way along the valley and is a splendid landmark.

Running northward to the East of the mountain are the twin valleys of East and West Baldwin. Many rivers and streams run into these valleys which empty their waters into the Injebreck Reservoir or on to the sea. It is likely that the Baldwins were awarded valley status because of their width.

GLENS

The glens of the Island with their narrow profiles far outnumber their larger neighbours. They vary in physical dimensions by length, breadth steepness, isolation, accessibility but not in beauty. Everyone of them has a grace of its very own. Give yourself time to reconnoitre and a favourite glen will present itself.

Many of the glens were only opened up to wheeled traffic because of the mining industry. One has to remember that the wheel only put in an appearance on the Island just over a couple of centuries ago. Pack horses and heavy wooden sledges were the main means of transporting goods about the countryside.

The rushing waters of the steep glens were put to good use for milling. Washing floors – for the extraction of minerals by water power; they were directed to drive turbines, in the manufacture of paper and the purity of the water favoured a number of attempts at setting up a cotton industry. There were many other manufacturing uses for the glens and every one will produce ancient buildings of one sort or another, sited to improve the economic well being of the Island. It is virtually impossible on a short visit to get anything but a flavour of the history of our glens.

In more modern times the glens have become centres for leisure and a thriving government

Mountains, Valleys, Glens and Parks

Injrebreck Reservoir

operated forestry industry. Many of the glens (seventeen) are owned by the Manx Government and in keeping with ancient rights you have free access to them. The Isle of Man Department of Agriculture, Fisheries and Forestry are responsible for the good husbandry of the public glens and they do a splendid job. A friendly word of advice if you decide on a bit of glen walking, please wear good shoes or trainers, the walking can be rough – the policy is to keep them as natural as possible. There is an excellent leaflet on glens available from the TIC's.

Our glens are divided into two types, the coastal glens and the mountain glens. Because the farmers until comparatively recent times used seaweed (locally called wrack) to fertilise their fields, access to beaches was essential and so you will find minor roads leading down to the sea. There are a number of very steep, thickly wooded, ravine like glens with no roads. These glens are found in the main on the East coast and mostly between Douglas and Ramsey. They usually have convenient car parks. The West coast glens are generally of a more gentle nature often leading down to sandy beaches. The mountain glens are very spectacular with tumbling streams and deep dark rocky pools. Care must always be taken when walking the mountain glens, the footpaths can often be very slippery, particularly after a period of rain. The more lush the vegetation the more likely you are to find huge rhododendron bushes giving marvellous splashes of colour to the most out of the way places.

PARKS

Parks almost seem to be a speciality of the Island. Many years ago the Founding Fathers of tourism took it upon themselves to build a great number of

Mountains, Valleys, Glens and Parks

parks in the towns and villages. Wherever you go on the Island you will find these peaceful oases of colour. Usually the parks are operated by the local authorities but there are a number that are looked after directly by the Department of Agriculture, Fisheries and Forestry.

Government parks such as the Arboretum at St John's are large and offer lovely well situated picnic areas. The park is full of trees and bushes, gifted to the Manx Nation by world governments in celebration of our Tynwald Millenium. Watch the friendly ducks however at the Arboretum, they are probably the best fed creatures on the Island and not at all adverse at reminding you of their presence. If you are in the vicinity of St John's a good suggestion is to visit the Department's nursery gardens. You are free to wander round the gardens and you will see why we are so proud of them… and of the good folk who work in all weathers throughout the year to give us endless hours of pleasure in the glens and parks.

Douglas has numerous parks and gardens and has always been fortuitous in having town councillors and a well led team of excellent gardeners who appreciate the pleasure the gardens give to the citizens of the Borough and visitors to the town alike. Pride of place has to be given to the "Sunken Gardens" on Douglas Promenade. Each year the gardens are virtually redesigned and special themes are used to celebrate anniversaries etc. Where else would you find a flower calender which changes date every day? A walk around the town will allow you to discover places like Hutchinson Square, Woodburn Square, Hilary Park all havens of tranquillity in the busy life of the town. Noble's Park along with the Villa Marina and its gardens was donated to the town by Henry Bloom Noble, and are renowned for their sporting facilities, offering bowls, tennis and many other leisure uses.

To the North end of Douglas Bay is Onchan Park. Endless fun for all the family and within walking distance of most of Douglas hotels or why not hop on a horse tram for a relaxing ride along the Promenade. At night the children love to walk down through Summer Hill Glen and delight in the fairy lights and illuminated animal displays.

Laxey has fine natural gardens and the children can have a wonderful time here. The site of the old mine washing floors have been turned into gardens to blend in with the surrounding landscape and offer good shelter on blustery days. Further North in Royal Ramsey, the very fine Mooragh Park awaits you. Mingled in with the flowers and bushes, its twelve acre shallow lake offers boating facilities for young and old. There are rowing boats, canoes, pedalos and sailing dinghies for hire or you can learn to sail, canoe or windsurf with one of the experienced instructors. All these facilities are provided by Mansail at the Boathouse. They also run the bowling green, crazy golf and the putting green. Not feeling energetic! Light refreshments and ices are available for those who just want to sit and watch.

A park with a difference is the Currraghs Wildlife Park near Ballaugh, on the A3. Set in natural surroundings the theme of the park allows visitors to wander amongst the enclosures, observing the animals and birds at close quarters. The cafe has a magnificent setting on the edge of a small lake with *Mount Karrin,* St Ciaran's Mount sitting guardian like above the Curraghs. Children love the Wildlife Park with its nature trails and there are play areas designed to let them work their surplus energy off.

This publication is the story of the origins of the World famous TT Races.

It tells of a car-crazy American in Europe, the clever secretary of what became the RAC and his cousin who was the Governor of the Isle of Man. It is a story of four and two wheeled development, of heroes, failures and great victories. Available from all leading bookshops in the Isle of Man at £6.95 or by mail order (£8.00 postage paid) from

Celt Marketing and Research, Abbey Ford, Ballasalla, Isle of Man.

SHEADINGS AND PARISHES

Dipping into the past always produces interesting facts and the Isle of Man is no exception. Proud to be the home of the oldest continuous Parliament in the world, the Island has many political differences from the adjacent countries. For instance there are no counties, instead ever since at least the 12th century, the Island was for administrative and political purposes traditionally divided into six sheadings. These Sheadings still exist to this very day and the derivation of the word is from the Gaelic *Seden* or, in more simplified form, six. Sheading is one of the few words still left in every day use from pre Viking days. In modern times, the Sheadings still have a political purpose with for example Rushen being represented by three members of the House of Keys.

The Isle of Man was divided ecclesiastically into seventeen parishes, each of which takes its name from a patron saint. Two parishes which at first glance do not conform to this are Jurby and Ballaugh. Further study of the subject shows that these names have been contracted from Kirk Patrick of Jurby and Kirk Mary of Ballaugh. Similarly Rushen and Lezayre are derived as shortened versions of Kirk Christ Rushen and Kirk Christ Lezayre. There is an argument that proclaims Rushen is named after St. Russin, one of the twelve Missionary Fathers, who along with St. Columba settled on the Island in the year 543 AD.

The six sheadings and their seventeen parishes are named as:

Ayre – Bride, Andreas and Lezayre.
Michael – Michael, Ballaugh and Jurby.
Glenfaba – Patrick, German and Marown.
Garff – Maughold and Lonan.
Middle – Onchan, Braddan and Santon.
Rushen – Rushen, Arbory and Malew.

For centuries now the sheadings have been drawn together, in a political sense, at the village of St. John's. Here stands the ancient Tynwald Hill or as it is called in Manx *Cronk Keeill Eoin* – Hill of St. John's Church. Legend tells us that the hill contains earth from all the seventeen ancient parishes, which would be in accordance with a known Norse practice.

There is evidence to suggest that the site was the centre for tribal gatherings and the proclamation of new rulers, well before the system of sheadings and parishes was introduced to the Isle of Man.

TRAVELLING TO THE ISLE OF MAN

Most people travelling to the Isle of Man treat the journey as the start of their holiday and approach it with a sense of adventure. After all visiting an island is not just a case of jumping into a car, finding the nearest convenient motorway and hoping for a trouble free drive. Islands by their very nature are isolated and it is this very isolation that in the past kept the Romans from finding us and the Normans from conquering us, and in more recent times vast hordes of tourists from visiting us. The very fact that there is a sea to cross has probably helped Ellan Vannin to preserve its peerless character and its unique atmosphere.

The gateways that the Island now enjoys means that travelling to our shores has become inevitably easier for the visitor. Connecting services by road and rail to the gateways has improved beyond recognition. Up to date information on all air and sea services can be obtained by contacting the various carriers direct or your local travel agent. As a useful tip, please note carefully, important information such as check in times for air and sea journeys, and you should also allow plenty of time to get safely to your chosen gateway. If you can, please try and book early, there are certain periods in the year when the Island is extremely busy and advanced booking is the only sure way of ensuring you get tickets for the journey of your choice.

The Isle of Man is fortunate in the way in which the two main carriers, the Isle of Man Steam Packet Company and Manx Airlines promote the Island. Much effort is expended by their staff in ensuring that the message of the attractiveness of the Isle of Man as a holiday destination is carried far and wide.

The Isle of Man Steam Packet Company operates a modern fleet of vessels and although founded in 1830, the company is still fiercely independent. During the summer months the sailings operate from six UK and Irish ports with the main all year round UK port being Heysham. Each of these gateways is served by good road and often by rail/bus connections, offering opportunities to reach the Island travelling as individuals, in family parties or in small to large groups. The Steam Packet have full

King Orry

Hoverspeed Experience the difference

Take a trip to France with Hoverspeed and you'll be spoilt for choice.

Will it be the dramatic, twin-hulled SeaCat, or the elegant hovercraft, at just 35 minutes the fastest service from Dover to Calais?

It's a tough call. Now, both SeaCat and hovercraft depart from the

Hoverport in Dover. So rest assured that whichever craft you choose, our exclusive port facilities mean a fast check-in and make queues or hold-ups a thing of the past.

For more information and booking details, see your travel agent or call direct on:
(0304) 240241

The New Wave.

Dover – Calais & Folkestone – Boulogne. Up to 26 return crossings per day.

booking facilities with British Rail which offer competitively priced fares from your local railway station… and if you are travelling in a group of ten or more by rail/sea or just by sea, ask for details of their special group fares. Should you wish the company to take the burden from you and arrange the total holiday then Magic Holidays – their package holiday division – will be more than happy to help.

Once on board the "King Orry" or the "Lady of Mann" the ships company's are at your service and each vessel is equipped with all the facilities and comforts you would expect to find on a modern ferry. The company is committed to offering you a first class service. There are on-board shopping facilities, where you can find a range of goods including daily papers, confectionery, games, souvenirs and much more. Travellers from the Republic of Ireland have the benefit of Duty Free shopping. Eating is no problem on board and a range of tasty foods and beverages is available on both ships.

Fresh sea air usually tires the kids out but just in case they still have some energy left, there are safe play areas available. For the older children there are the latest video games to enjoy and as they gradually slow down they can take in a free film or cartoon in the cinema. Any queries, please ask the friendly staff at the Information Bureau, they will be glad to help.

Travelling to the Isle of Man by air has never been easier with Manx Airlines operating direct services from no less than thirteen UK and Irish gateways. Additionally there are a number of other hub airports throughout the British Isles and Europe which offer onward connections to the Island.

Established in November 1982, Manx Airlines soon proved that it could provide a complimentary service to the sea carrier and although in direct competition with each other, both companies do work together for the benefit of the Isle of Man. The modern fleet of aircraft, including British Aerospace 146 jets, British Aerospace ATPs (Advanced Turboprop), Shorts SD – 360s and British Aerospace Jetstreams ensure their passengers are carried in comfort and speed to the Island. The distinctive livery of the aircraft ensure that they are easily recognised and the strong affinity with all things Manx is emphasised by the national motif on the tail, and the words *skianyn vannin*, Wings of Man, near the front of the aircraft.

Manx Airlines have always worked hard to involve package holiday operators in their plans and if you require this type of holiday there are a number of ways of achieving it. Elsewhere in the guide are adverts from local package holiday operators and it is suggested that contact with one or other of them is the best way of getting up to date information. None of the flights take any great length of time to bring the happy tourist here, so if you can wait until your first meal on the Isle of Man, then please make do with the very good free in-flight meal or snack provided.

Group travel is available with Manx and they love to carry golfers over to play the excellent courses, but be sure that you let them know in good time to help them make the appropriate arrangements for your clubs. If you are flying from Manchester and travelling out from the city centre, the new rail link certainly helps Manx Airlines passengers make the right connection.

Geographically the Island is ideally situated to receive visitors from the closer parts of the British Isles but increasingly, we are being discovered by tourists from further afield and all parts of the globe. To assist in planning your journey to the Isle of Man an indication of travel distances and times from the gateways is provided.

Sea journey distance in miles (crossing times in hours and minutes) to the Isle of Man:

Ardrossan 106 (8.00)   Dublin 82 (4.45)
Fleetwood 56 (3.20)   Belfast 79 (4.45)
Heysham 59 (3.45)   Liverpool 73 (4.00)

Flight distance in miles and time (in minutes) are for direct travel to the Isle of Man:

Belfast 62 (30)   Leeds/Bradford 122 (55)
Birmingham 162 (60)   Liverpool 88 (30)
Blackpool 68 (30)   London Heathrow 251 (60)
Cardiff 193 (60)   Luton 234 (70)
Dublin 79 (30)   Manchester 108 (40)
Glasgow 124 (50)   Newcastle 133 (60)
Jersey 352 (135)

TOWNS AND VILLAGES

DOUGLAS

Distances Ballasalla 9m, Castletown 12m, Laxey 8m, Peel 11m, Port Erin 15, Port St Mary 16m, Ramsey 16m.

The Isle of Man's front door is Douglas, nestling in the gentle curve of Douglas Bay. The best place to observe the Island's capital is from the top of Douglas Head. The whole of Douglas Bay, as far as Onchan Head, is spread out before you with the promenades and a seemingly endless line of hotels and guesthouses stretching away from you. Fringed by gardens to the front and with a backdrop of Snaefell, it is one of the most striking bays in Europe. On a fine summer's eve, Douglas wears its illuminations like a necklace. Thousands of jewel-like lights spread out over nearly two miles between the Heads of the Bay, one of the greatest free shows on earth.

On the twin piers, millions of holiday makers have arrived in the elegant vessels of the Isle of Man Steam Packet Company. From these same piers, thousands of Manx have sailed away to a new life, while others departed by steamer to fight for King and country, some never to see their fair Isle again. Throughout the reigns of seven monarchs, this fine company has given over one hundred and sixty years of unbroken service to the Island. The harbour has witnessed lots of changes in the last decade and a half, after many years of standing still. How many people know that the King Edward Pier is the only public work or building named after the uncrowned sovereign? On leaving the gates of the Victoria Pier, how many people notice the memorial to the only working man in the history of the Island to have a public monument erected to his bravery? The "Dawsey" memorial commemorates the brave acts of David "Dawsey" Kewley, a ropeman with the Isle of Man Steam Packet Company, who was reputed to have saved no less than thirty five men from drowning.

Emptying fresh water into the inner harbour is the Douglas River, which gives the town its name, but only flows from the eastern end of the National Sports

Douglas

Centre in the King George V Park. Two rivers, the Dhoo and the Glass join as one at this spot and the rest, as they say, is history. To learn more about the town a visit to the Museum is a must; any attempt to precis the story of Douglas would be derisory on the part of the author. It is far better for those who seek in-depth knowledge of the town to enjoy the process of information seeking at the Museum.

One of the most historically important buildings in the Isle of Man is the Castle Mona. Operating now as a hotel, this elegant Regency style building has moved on from being the home of the Duke of Atholl to being a leader in the hotel and entertainment industry. Future plans include a ten pin bowling alley and its night club Jimmy B's is a firm favourite with the young. This is a company that is going places.

Next door neighbour is the Palace Hotel. It takes more than a few words to describe what the Palace has to offer, but wherever you go in the world people have heard of this famous hotel, and it is not unusual for people to part company on a foreign shore with the words "See you in the Palace Round Bar". The Renaissance Health Club and all its associated facilities are available for guests of the Palace, and there is no excuse for you to go home in anything but the best of health, but you do have to promise to try the culinary delights served up by the head chef and his team. The fine facilities of this modern complex are packaged through their in-house travel company, Group and Conference Travel, or you can book direct with the hotel… and if you feel like a gamble,

Douglas

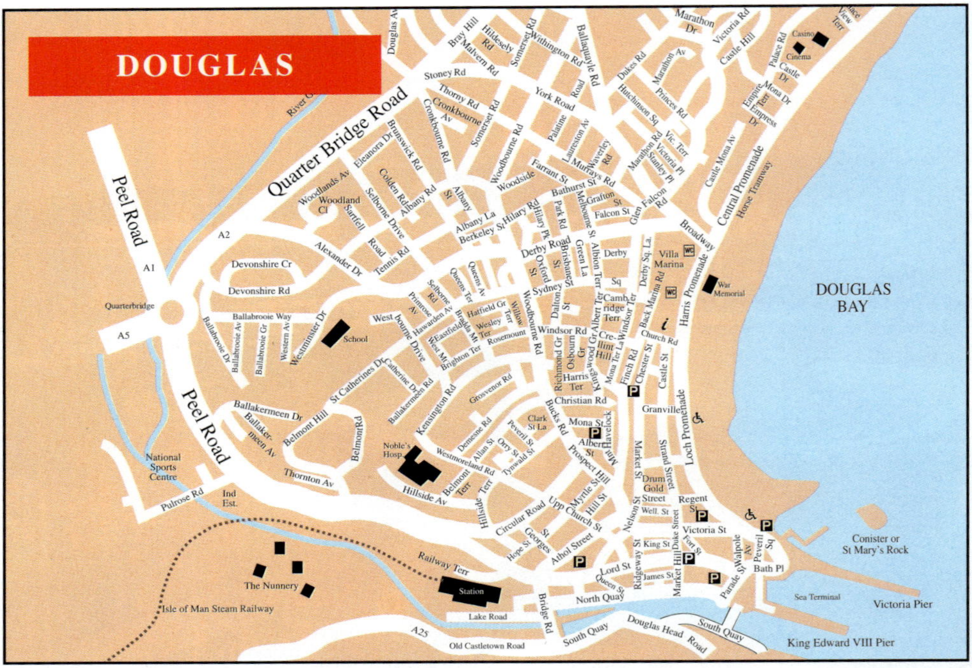

DOUGLAS

(map of Douglas, Isle of Man)

The Island's Most Elegant Hotel
THE CASTLE MONA HOTEL

♛♛♛♛♛
Highly Commended

Built in 1801 as the home of the 4th Duke of Athol and turned into an hotel in 1835, the Castle Mona has now been tastefully restored to its original splendour, yet offering all the modern facilities and comforts of an International Standard Hotel. As one of the Island's finest buildings, the Castle Mona commands an enviable location on the promenade overlooking Douglas Bay, and yet is only minutes away from the main shopping and commercial areas.

Luxurious Bedrooms with private bathrooms
4 Suites, with Jacuzzi Bath – 2 with Four-Poster beds
Dickens Bar, furnished with leather Chesterfields, offers live music at weekends.
Regency Restaurant offering the finest food at competitive prices, and served in elegant surroundings. Grand Ballroom with original 30 ft high hand painted ceiling and crystal chandeliers boasts frequent dinner dances also within the complex.

Superior accommodation at budget prices

MANX SUPERBOWL   Jimmy B's Nightclub

Central Promenade, Douglas, Isle of Man
Tel: 0624 624540 Fax 0624 675360

it has the only Casino on the Island.

Postcards are an integral part of any holiday and the Island is lucky that it has a wide choice. Please remember though that besides our own currency, we have our own postage stamps. Several times each year the Isle of Man Post Office issues sets of new Definitive Stamps. Nigel Mansell OBE was honoured with a set of two stamps late in 1992, and in January 1993 the set depicted ships associated with the Island. Stamp collecting has always been a popular hobby with young and old. The Island's stamps offer not only the opportunity to extend a collection but, in addition, they can be valuable souvenirs or presents from your holiday. In case you need to phone home, Manx Telecom operate the same system of phones that you are used to back in the UK, however you will need to purchase one of their colourful phone cards for on Island use when using a Cardphone… and they are nice to keep as souvenirs.

The world famous TT races in June each year, supported by the Manx Grand Prix in August, flood the Island with thousands of bikers and race enthusiasts. The nice thing about the races is the friendly club atmosphere that it generates. For those who are unaware of the races and their historical connections with the Isle of Man, they have been running since 1907, and car races were even earlier than that. Steve Hislop's book "You Couldn't Do It Now!" is an excellent publication to help set out the background to the TT. Douglas has always played the leading role in the races and a visit to the TT Grandstand is a must, particularly at race times. Fans have their own particular favourite places to stay and return year after year, often becoming family friends with the hoteliers.

On Loch Promenade there are a number of well known family run hotels, all offering friendly personal service to their guests. The Cunard Hotel has all the facilities you would associate with a hotel of this size and there is no need to go out for an evening meal, they provide delicious dinners. The Quirk family provide reduced rates for children, groups and OAPs, and if you are a golfer, you have chosen the right place to stay. Close neighbour is the Ellan Vannin Hotel, run by the Collisters. The first thing you notice is the wonderful display of flowers at the front entrance, which has won for the hotel the "Douglas in Bloom" competition many times.

Ellan Vannin
31 Loch Promenade, Douglas
Commended   **Private Hotel**

"Douglas in Bloom" competition winners
1988-1989-1991-1992

For 22 years we have had a reputation for being spotlessly clean, offering good old fashioned hospitality, excellent food, personal service and a homely atmosphere. What better recipe for a successful holiday.

- TV Lounge ■ Snooker Room ■ Full Central Heating
- All Bedrooms en-suite ■ With Satellite TV,
- Tea/Coffee Facilities ■ Private telephone
- Non-smoking dining room ■ No licensed bar

Telephone/Fax: (0624) 674824

CUNARD HOTEL
Friendly, family run hotel,
close to town and beaches.
◆ Most bedrooms en-suite
◆ Varied Menus ◆ Warm friendly bar
◆ Reduced rates for children,
OAPs & Party Bookings
28/29 LOCH PROM, DOUGLAS
Tel: 0624 676728 Fax: 0624 676728

Melrose
A FAMILY RUN HOTEL IN GOOD LOCATION
TO TOWN CENTRE AND BEACHES.
• Open all Year
• Modern well appointed rooms most
with private facilities and TV's
• Good Home Cooking
• Comfortable Lounges
LOCH PROMENADE, DOUGLAS
TELEPHONE: (0624) 676269

SEFTON HOTEL

The Sefton Hotel is more than an attractive, friendly five crown commended hotel, it is the complete all year round Island holiday; bringing you the best possible inclusive travel, hotel facilities, good food and drink with an exciting range of holiday experiences to choose from - all at very competitive prices.

Relish the superb cuisine, prepared from the highest quality produce and served with real draught ales and quality wines at sensible prices. Whether you are in the mood for the carvery, grill room menu or a light afternoon snack, you can enjoy a succulent roast with all the trimmings, a vegetarian delight or a round of freshly made sandwiches in the **Far Pavilions** or the **Harris Coffee and Cocktail Lounge.**

The luxury **Fountain Health Club** includes a swimming pool, jacuzzi, relaxing poolside bar, gymnasium, steam rooms, saunas, sunbed rooms and a beauty therapy room.

The **Tramshunters** is the hotel's own CAMRA highly recommended pub with the widest range of real ales on the Island and beyond - and a selection of pub lunches to match.

INSTANT FULLY INCLUSIVE QUOTES AVAILABLE BY CALLING THE INFORMATION HOTLINE 663320

The Sefton is the perfect place from which to enjoy the Island.

All 80 attractive ensuite bedrooms have satellite TV, Teletext, direct dial phones, hairdryers and tea/coffee making facilities. Our Family Suites provide you the luxury of privacy with a separate children's bedroom.

The Discovery Guide Visitor Centre provides a fascinating selection of daily holiday options for you to choose from:

Visit the Calf of Man seals, puffins, Manx shearwaters and choughs by boat, make your stage entrance through the hotel's secret door into the Victorian Gaiety Theatre, visit the world's oldest parliament, see the "Story of Mann" - all provide an insight into the history, culture, charm and beauty of this magic Isle.

HARRIS PROMENADE · DOUGLAS · ISLE OF MAN · IM1 2RW · TEL: 0624 626011 · FAX: 0624 676004

Recognising that green fingers are not enough, Eddie and Margaret have built up a reputation spanning almost a quarter of a century for good old fashioned hospitality, and you are offered a home from home atmosphere all year round. What better recipe for a successful holiday. The Melrose Hotel is within walking distance of the Sea Terminal and the Howards make sure that everything you need to make your stay enjoyable, is to hand. Keen on families, all the little extras are provided for the youngsters and there are baby listening facilities. Group reductions are available and the bar is open to midnight. For many years now the Windsor Hotel has been run by the Creevy family. Their speciality is to ensure that you relax on holiday and if your desire is to fish, golf, walk or just get away from it all, they are the people to help. Travel packages including special rates for parties can be arranged. Personal supervision is important to the Manx hotel industry and the Rio Hotel complies with that rule. The Ireton family hotel is close to all the town facilities and offers the guest everything they would expect to find in a much larger operation. Besides normal meals, you can enjoy snacks, and all rooms have satellite TV.

Inner Harbour – Douglas

Douglas has many sides to it, far too many to describe in a publication of this nature. Informal entertainment there is in plenty with many of the pubs putting on musical entertainment, such as Caseys Cafe Bar. Formal entertainment in Douglas centres on the beautifully restored Gaiety Theatre. Throughout the year plays, pantomimes, concerts, last night of the proms and a veritable myriad of shows, delight audiences. Opened for its first performance in July 1900, the Gaiety soon won a place in the hearts of the locals and tourists, to the degree that it is now considered to be a national treasure. Frank Matcham, the famous Victorian theatre architect would be pleased that over ninety years later his work still stands, largely unaltered, as a monument to his skills. In Government ownership, the management and staff are assisted by an enthusiastic band of helpers known as "The Friends of the Gaiety". Up to date films can be seen at Summerland's Piazza Cinema or in one or the other of the Palace Cinemas.

Enjoyment of your holiday is important and whatever the weather you can be assured that Summerland, the entertainment centre of Douglas will have something to suit everyone. As well as the cinema with the latest Dolby Sound System, each summer during the peak of the season family shows are performed daily. Should the children become bored there is a large supervised play area and if they really want to burn off the calories, the sports facilities at Summerland are superb. Roller skating, squash, badminton and table tennis, are just a few of the participant sports that are available. All the sporting activities are supported with showers, saunas etc, but if you really want to cool off then a quick dash next door to the Derby Castle Aquadrome will do the trick. Open seven days a week, the thirty three metre main pool and trainer pool give hours of fun and are well supervised. For a real holiday treat, there are Turkish and Russian baths, saunas, sunbeds and an Aerotone Spa.

The Harris Promenade is home not only to the Gaiety Theatre but to the Sefton Hotel. Immediately next to the front door of the theatre is the Discovery

PALACE HOTEL & CASINO

Central Promenade, Douglas, Isle of Man
Tel: (0624) 662662 Fax: (0624) 670848

For Business or Pleasure - choose the Palace Hotel - the No 1 hotel in Douglas for facilities

£ Multi Million Leisure Club
(free to residents)

Nightclub (free to residents)

2 Luxury Cinemas

2 Casinos and Bingo Hall
(with instant membership)

Bars open until 3.30am

Executive Rooms and Suites

Meetings for up to 300 delegates

Seafront Location

Travel inclusive packages available through our 'in-house' bonded Tour Operator:
Group and Conference Travel, Central Promenade, Douglas, Isle of Man Tel: (0624) 662000

3266

Outdoor facilities for all the family

- Nobles Park offers 3 Crown Bowling Greens, TT Crazy Golf, Putting, Tennis, 18 Hole Miniature Golf, Kiddies Tot-Lot and Children's Playground
- Pulrose Golf Course – 18 holes with a Professional in attendance
- Villa Marina Gardens, spacious & sheltered
- Summer Hill Glen with Illuminated Fairy Glen (July to September)
- Award winning Sunken Promenade Gardens
- Grandstand Campsite (not available TT fortnight)

Camping & General Enquiries Tel: 621132

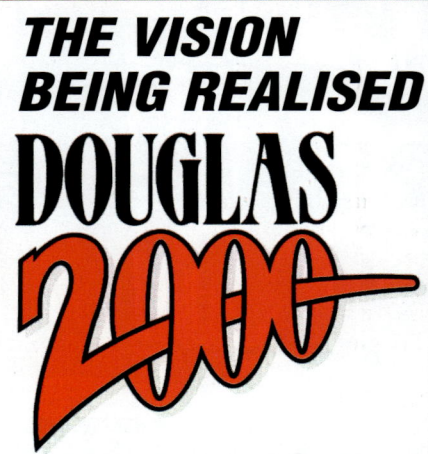

THE VISION BEING REALISED

DOUGLAS 2000

DOUGLAS 2000 CENTRE
34 VICTORIA STREET
DOUGLAS
TEL: (0624) 670600

GAIETY THEATRE

SOMETHING FOR EVERYONE

*Plays, Pantomimes, Concerts throughout the year.
Ring now to book and for full season details:-*

Tel: (0624) 625001

Guide Visitor Centre. The centre provides all sorts of valuable information to the tourist and one particularly useful product is The Isle of Man Guide… Where to eat, what to do, where to go, the best pubs, where to find the cash points, some of the nicest picnic spots, the most interesting walks, shops you shouldn't miss, beautiful churches, lovely gardens, fascinating guided tours, car hire, coach tours, maps, making the most of the Island's unique transport system, what's on, an entertainment guide, help lines, afternoon tea at its best, days to remember, and much more… and all backed up by the Discovery Guide Visitor Centre. The Isle of Man Pocket Guide is available throughout the Island.

Moving further along we come to Central Promenade. Its most distinctive feature is the strikingly attractive Empress Hotel. The Empress has always been an industry leader and under new ownership it has been completely re-built. It had the distinction in 1992 of being the first hotel on the Isle of Man to be awarded the Five Crowns, Highly Commended rating; an award the management and staff are extremely proud of. Justifying this high grading is easy, the hotel has every conceivable form

Isle of Man Government Offices

IMPERIAL HOTEL
Central Promenade, Douglas
Tel: 0624 621656 Fax: 0624 672160

Family run hotel is ideally situated in the centre of Douglas Promenade
- 60 comfortable bedrooms many en-suite and all having TV & tea/coffee facilities
- Two passenger lifts ● Lounge Bar
- Live Entertainment on certain evenings
- Good home style cooking
- Parties catered for all year

♛♛♛ Commended

Edwina Ely

China and Gifts at affordable prices
◆ Spode   ◆ I.O.M. Railway Plates
◆ Noritake   ◆ Belleek
◆ Linen   ◆ Paperweights
18 St Paul's Square, Ramsey
Tel: 814004   Mail Order Available

FERNLEIGH
Is Different

A family run Victorian detached house, set in own grounds with panoramic views of Douglas Bay.
PARKING, GARAGE, GARDEN, COMFORTABLE EN-SUITE & ECONOMY BEDROOMS WITH TEA MAKING FACILITIES, RADIO & TV.

BED & BREAKFAST FROM £15.00 daily

Enquires to: Jennifer Hall, Fernleigh, Palace Road, Douglas
Tel: 0624 675553   ♛♛Crown Approved

IN 1993 ALMOST 2,000,000 SHOPPERS VISITED THE STRAND

"Shopping in Douglas is so much better with the Strand!"

At the Strand Shopping Centre, you'll find the best names in shopping side by side in the perfect place to shop...

Dorothy Perkins . . . Stead and Simpson . . . Dash . . . Fizz . . . Fagins . . . Body Shop . . . Mother-care . . . Evans . . . Perzazz . . .

Tandy . . . The Mall Café . . . Birthdays . . . Harrison Musique . . . Ideal Home . . . Strand Toys . . .

You can take time to enjoy your shopping at the Strand - you are indoors, and with the panoramic lift and escalators, getting around the Centre is so easy.

THE **S T R A N D**
SHOPPING CENTRE
Your Shopping's in the Bag!

of comfort and facility for their guests. Ranging from every one of the luxurious bedrooms with its own marble bathroom, to the health club with its indoor swimming pool and on to the international cuisine of La Brasserie, the Empress gives full value for money... and if you are not satisfied, they offer a money back guarantee of satisfaction. Now that is confidence for you!

In a different category to the Empress but matching it for the warmth of service is the family run Imperial Hotel. Shirley, Derek, Jeanne and David with years of experience between them, manage this popular hotel. Home cooked meals, the bars, reception, bedrooms etc all benefit from the hands on management of the family. Golfers find kindred spirits at the Imperial and if you want a group holiday give them a ring, they can arrange all sorts of packages and deals. The sole aim of the Imperial team is to make your holiday a memorable one. Parking in strange towns can often cause problems for tourists. The Fernleigh in Palace Road, perched on the cliff top with sweeping views of Douglas Bay has no such worries. This comfortable, family run Victorian House offers peaceful, stress free holidays... and no worries about the car!

Leaving Central Promenade behind, you come to the Queens Promenade. Quite a number of public bars are along this end of town, the Queens Hotel being a good example. Selling Okell's bitter, they can't serve it fast enough in busy periods such as the TT, and if you like railway nostalgia, the Terminus Tavern is the place for you. The early morning sunshine brings out the early risers and many visitors sit outside their hotels enjoying the sun and reading their newspapers before eating a hearty Manx breakfast. The owners of the Silvercraigs Hotel, Moira and Michael Spenser, have built up a high reputation for this well known seafront hotel. The Manx tradition of hospitality extends to giving the holiday maker a warm welcome and lots of careful care and attention during their stay, and it manifests itself nowhere better than at the Silvercraigs. Ideally situated for the Manx Electric Railway, just a few minutes' walk, there are equally no car parking problems at this end of the Promenade.

There are various methods of booking holidays to the Isle of Man, some of which have been mentioned elsewhere. Everymann Holidays is probably the

Villa Marina
HARRIS PROMENADE DOUGLAS
ISLE OF MAN TEL (0624) 74171

Family Cabaret shows throughout the summer.
Various star Arts in the Royal Hall
See billboard for details or telephone 628855
Refreshments

Spacious Entertainment Centre in the heart of Douglas
Award Winning, Spacious, shelted gardens

King Edward Road, Douglas,
Isle of Man.
SPORTS FACILITIES
Squash, Badminton, 5-a-side,
Basketball, Saunas and Sunbeds
CINEMA
Open 7 days a week

CHILDREN'S PLAY AREA
Slides, Bouncy Castles, Ball Pool etc.
*A FULL CABARET SHOWING
NIGHTLY DURING THE SUMMER
SEASON. ENTERTAINMENT FOR
ALL THE FAMILY.*
CAVE NIGHTCLUB
Open 9pm – 2am. Fridays: "Up Front Music". Saturdays: Golden Oldies Music from the 60's and 70's
For further information tel (0624) 625511

AQUADROME

33 METRE MAIN POOL

12 METRE LEARNER POOL

SPA SUITE

TURKISH - SAUNA - SUNBEDS - AERETONE - BUBBLE TUBS

**SUMMERTIME FUN
CHUTE SESSIONS AND FRIDAY
FUN NIGHTS**

Programme varies through the year. To avoid disappointment
**Phone (0624) 673411.
DERBY CASTLE AQUADROME: DOUGLAS, ISLE OF MAN**

largest Manx based company offering package holidays to the Island. Everymann is the Department of Tourism's very own tour operator and it combines the best of quality, value and choice to suit most budgets. The skilled staff working in Centaurmann House, Duke Street, have a comprehensive knowledge of the industry and are quickly able to match up your requirements to availability. Booking your holiday with Everymann benefits you in all sorts of ways. The size of the operation means that it can negotiate the best deals on your behalf with the carriers, you may also benefit from special discounts, reduced admissions and other concessions. Continual vetting of the product means that it maintains its high standards.

Travel Services Isle of Man, based at Irwell House on Harris Promenade, are market leaders for holiday packages, providing many different opportunities for the prospective visitor. For example, their facilities allow last minute bookings. Their use of Tele Text and a central reservation service means that you can quickly decide on the Isle of Man as a destination and with one phone call achieve a booking. TSL work directly with many of the hotels, guest houses and self catering apartments, and by indicating your preferred travel arrangements to the establishment of your choice, packages can be quickly arranged through the operator.

One of the oldest companies in the Isle of Man and one which is very much involved in tourism is Okell's Limited, Brewers of traditional bitter and mild beers. This fine old company has not let time stand still for them since they brewed their first beer in 1850 and they are now the proud owners of a new complex at Kewaigue on the outskirts of Douglas. One of the prime aims of the company is to ensure customer comfort and their refurbishment programme is continuous. The famous Quarterbridge Hotel, and

Molly's Kitchen and Tavern in Onchan, are but two of many hotels throughout the Island that have benefited from this visionary planning. Catering for generations of visitors, their name is synonymous with real ales which have long since disappeared from elsewhere in the British Isles. Their distinctive symbol is known by Islanders as the "Okell's Falcon". They have numerous pubs, inns, and hotels spread all over the Island so, if you fancy a pint or two, look for the falcon and be assured of quality. A suggestion that might start you on the Real Ale Trail is to visit the "Barbary Coast". No, you have not left the Isle of Man, it is the local nickname for the pubs along the North Quay. Good luck in your quest and remember, "Okell's, the taste that's stood the test of time".

No vacation is complete without taking photographs and visitors are always impatient to see the results. Ian and Monica Clark run Island Photographics, where those vivid reminders of the holiday can be processed. Their shop and laboratory are conveniently situated in Castle Street, not too far from the Gaiety Theatre and the Tourist Information Centre. If you need any suggestions or assistance with your photographic requirements, ask at the shop – they will be only too pleased to help.

Shopping in Douglas is easy with the majority of shops situated behind Loch Promenade and running into Duke Street at the harbour end of town. Great plans are afoot for developing Douglas but the Strand Shopping Centre showing faith in the Island is already in full swing, and with almost two million shoppers visiting the "Strand", their confidence has

---

THE WINDSOR HOTEL
DOUGLAS

Situated in the heart of Douglas on the seafront. Pleasant hotel withGood Food. Spacious Lounges. Games Room. Coffee Shop. Wide selection of Bedrooms. Lift. Night Porter.
Send for colour brochure – enquiries to A.D. Creevey
Loch Promenade, Douglas
Telephone: (0624) 676169/676169

THE RIO HOTEL, DOUGLAS

Good home cooked food. Choice Menu. Dining Room is a no smoking area. Most rooms en-suite. All rooms have Sky TV, Radios and Tea making facilities. B&B and B&B Eve. Meal available. Licensed Bar. Two Crown Approved.

42 Loch Promenade, Douglas
Tel: (0624) 623491 Fax: (0624) 670966

Don't Take A Chance With Your Holiday, Stay At The Island's Premier Hotel.

For a free Empress Hotel brochure and details of our All Inclusive Packages by air and sea, call now. Please quote Ref 10G2.

FREEFONE 0800 585060

A Better Understanding

HIGHLY COMMENDED

The Empress Hotel, Central Promenade, Douglas, Isle of Man. IM2 4RA. Telephone (0624) 661155 Fax (0624) 673554

been repaid. Many of the familiar store names from the UK are present. You can buy a full variety of goods here ranging from leading fashions, shoes, toiletries, babyware, books, electrical and household equipment, music and video tapes, greetings cards, fancy goods, toys, and even a new "hairdo". If you are hungry, try The Mall Cafe – they have a wide selection of snacks and meals. The Centre also hosts exhibitions, band concerts and charitable events throughout the year.

What does the future hold for Douglas in this ever-changing world of ours? This was a question posed a number of years ago in an attempt to plan the town's progress into the twenty first century. As a result, Douglas 2000 was born. Douglas 2000 is a Partnership of the Isle of Man Government, Douglas Corporation, the Chamber of Commerce and local companies working together to improve the environment and economy of the Island capital.

The Partnership has embarked upon a programme of more than one hundred projects to make Douglas a successful town well equipped for the twenty first century. Plans include eight "Flagship" projects to bring about improvements to the shopping

SILVERCRAIGS HOTEL
Queens Promenade, Douglas.
TEL: (0624) 674903

Superbly situated close to all amenities and opposite the beach, this popular Manx owned hotel has a high reputation for service and excellent cuisine.
- All Bedrooms en suite with satellite TV
- Open all year
- Full Central Heating
- Lift ● Parking

Send for our colour brochure today

  ☆☆APPROVED

An Equine Sanctuary

VISIT OUR RETIRED TRAM HORSES and DONKEYS
- Free Admission
- Free Car Park
- Museum & Cafe
- Souvenir Shop

Voted Top Tourist Attraction 1993
Home of Rest for Old Horses

3 miles from Douglas, main Airport Road. Buses stop at the door
Open Mon to Wed from last week in May to the middle of September
10.00am to 5.00pm
BULRHENNY, RICHMOND HILL, DOUGLAS TEL: 674594

streetscape, promenade, Villa Marina, Villiers, and off street parking, and achieve a town square, yacht harbour, and development zone. If you want to know more about these exciting plans, contact the Douglas 2000 Centre, 34 Victoria Street, Douglas, IM1 2LB, telephone (0624) 670600.

Public Amenities
Coastguard (Officer in Charge) (0624) 661664
General Post Office, Regent Street (0624) 620666
Douglas Corporation (Town Hall) (0624) 623021
Nobles (IOM) Hospital (0624) 663322
Police Station (0624) 631212
Emergency Only –
Fire, Police, Ambulance, Coastguard 999
Banks
Bank of Ireland (IOM), Christian Road
  (0624) 661102 Bank of Scotland (IOM),
  Prospect Hill (0624) 623074
Barclays, Victoria Street (0624) 682000
Isle of Man Bank, Athol Street (0624) 626232
Lloyds, Prospect Hill (0624) 625614
Midland, Victoria Street (0624) 623051
National Westminster, Prospect Hill (0624) 629292

Royal Bank of Scotland (IOM), Prospect Hill
  (0624) 629111
TSB Bank, Strand Street (0624) 673755
Building Societies
Alliance & Leicester (IOM), Prospect Hill
  (0624) 663566
Bradford & Bingley (IOM), Ridgeway Street
  (0624) 661868
Britannia (IOM), Victoria Street (0624) 628512
Leeds Permanent, Strand Street (0624) 626266
N & P Overseas, Strand Street (0624) 662244
Nationwide Overseas, Athol Street (0624) 663494
Leisure Centres
Aquadrome (0624) 673411
Summerland (0624) 625511
Tourist Information
Current Flight Information (0624) 600600
Douglas Corporation Horsetrams (0624) 675222
Flight Information (0624) 824354
Harbour Control (0624) 686628
Isle of Man Railways (Steam & Electric)
  (0624) 663366
Isle of Man Steam Packet Company (0624) 661661
Isle of Man Transport (0624) 662525
Jersey European Airways (0624) 822162
Manx Airlines (0624) 824313
Museum, Manx National Heritage (0624) 675522
Ronaldsway Airport General Enquiries
  (0624) 823311
Tourist Information Centre (0624) 686766

Manx Telecom Phonecards

A highly collectable and practical way to keep in touch. Available from shops and Post Offices throughout the Island
**Queen Victoria House,
Victoria Street,
Douglas, Isle of Man.**
Manx Telecom

Discover the Isle of Man

with a guided excursion on one of our modern coaches – or on a nostalgic trip on one of our vintage models. Either way we can be of service. Please contact our main office at Summerhill or our booking office on Central Promenade.
Telephone Douglas 674301 or 676105.
Parties and Groups catered for.

TOURS [ISLE OF MAN]

Coach Hire • Inclusive Tours • Excursions • Ground Handling

BALLASALLA

Distances Castletown 3m, Douglas 9m, Laxey 17m, Peel 10m, Port Erin 6m, Port St Mary 7m, Ramsey 24m.

Ballasalla lies in the parish of Malew within the Sheading of Rushen. Flowing gently through the area is the Silverburn river and it is from this river that the village received its name. It is probable that *Salla* or *Sallach* was the ancient Gaelic name by which the early inhabitants knew the river; translated into English it means "the village of the sally or willow river". A more modern Gaelic translation of Silverburn is *Awin Argid* or "Silver River".

The village is served by a regular bus service and during the summer months, nothing is better than to travel there by steam train. The line to Ballasalla is part of the 1873/4 built railway, connecting Douglas and Port Erin. However in 1986 a brand new station was built on the opposite side of the track to make way for an imposing set of offices which provide excellent employment opportunities for the people of the village. One of the beneficial aspects of business life in the Isle of Man is the efforts made by all sections of the economy to work together. At Ballasalla Station, you can witness this at first hand as you alight from the train onto the first new railway station to be built in the best part of a century. Crossleys the Accountants of Ballasalla are very proud to be the donors of this fine new addition to the railway. The office being situated alongside the track is of course a tremendous bonus for clients, who can pop out on the train to see their Accountants... and the parking is pretty easy as well. If you need your finances taking care of, you might well find an exploratory meeting with these enthusiastic supporters of the Railway worthwhile.

Settled in early times Ballasalla has played its part in the making of Manx history. Within its boundaries lie the ruins of Rushen Abbey, said to have been founded in 1098 by Magnus, King of Norway. The building of the Abbey commenced in 1134 and although, as with many ancient sites, it was utilised over the centuries as a ready made source of building materials, much of the original buildings remain. Adjoining the ruins is the Rushen Abbey Hotel run by the husband and wife team of Ray and Peggy Griffin. You can sample fine ales and lagers here or

Rushen Abbey

if you would just like a coffee or tea, that's on hand as well. On a fine day the busiest spot is outside the hotel and if the kids are feeding the ducks, make sure they don't get anything more than their feet wet.

There have been many exciting discoveries made during excavations at the Abbey. Records show that a number of Kings and Abbots lie buried within its precincts and an excavation in the early part of this century discovered a skeleton of a man buried with a bronze figure representing Osiris an Egyptian God, which points to his having been a Crusader.

The *Chronicon Manniae,* "Chronicles of Mann", a valuable reference work for the early history of the Island, were written at Rushen Abbey. Contained within the "Chronicles" is an account of the murder by a Knight called Ivar of Reginald II, King of Mann. But the Monks were busy in other areas as well, draining the land, straightening the course of the local rivers and streams, and generally influencing the way of life in those far off times. One valuable example of their handiwork still remains in every day use a few yards upstream from the Abbey Gardens. Known as the Monk's Bridge, its Gaelic name was *Crossag,* the little cross or crossing, and it still carries people over the Silverburn river. Dating from the twelfth century and only 3½ feet wide, it is one of the finest examples of a packhorse bridge

Crossleys

Certified Acccountants and
Registered Auditors

*"Personal Attention Given from
People Who Care About You"*

P.O. Box 1
Portland House,
Station Road,
Ballasalla,
Isle of Man.

Tel: +44 (0)624 822816
Fax: +44 (0)624 824570

Rushen Abbey Hotel

Lunches served 6 days a week 12-2pm
REASONABLE PRICES
VARIED MENU
Friendly atmosphere and children welcome
LIVE MUSIC EVERY SATURDAY
Snacks - Tea - Coffee - All Day

to be found anywhere in the British Isles.

Just a little further upstream from the bridge, the Silverburn is joined by the *Awin Ruy,* or Red River, whose bed is strewn with boulders as it flows down from *Rozefel,* Granite Mountain. Nowadays this mountain is called Stoney Mountain and it was from this source that much of the building materials came for the building of the new Douglas Breakwater in 1979. The Norsemen also recognised the colouring of the granite as it was exposed to the elements and knew it as *Rjoofjall,* Ruddy Mountain. Completing the short walk up from the Abbey to Silverdale Glen is a very pleasant experience, much loved by all ages and on the way… look out for the Wishing Well.

There is much to recommend the visitor to Silverdale. Originally the site of the Creg Mill, its dam is now used as a boating lake. Utilising spare parts has always been a profitable pastime for the Manx and the water-powered roundabout is no exception. By using one of the old Foxdale mines water wheels and an ingenious method of gearing, generations of children "of all ages" have enjoyed themselves on this unique system. The beautifully kept cafe serves snacks and meals all day throughout

MORE THAN JUST A DAY OUT

- CAFE
- PARK
- MERRY - GO - ROUND
- PLAYGROUND
- WALKS
- TRAILS

Silverdale Glen, Ballasalla, Isle of Man.

Telephone (0624) 823474

OPEN EVERY DAY EASTER - SEPTEMBER
9.00 am - 5.30 pm

a long season and there is often a special event to amuse everyone, no matter how old or young. .

Ballasalla in the days of the Cistercians was very much a commercial centre for the Island and so it is today with Ronaldsway Airport falling within its boundaries. What the ancestors of today's villagers would think of the aeroplane is best left to the imagination. Ronaldsway lies a little to the South of the village and can be reached by bus or taxi and although there is a railway halt nearby, this is now rarely if ever used. Given its name by the early Scandinavian visitors and meaning "Reginald's Ford", there were several Manx kings of this name. Within the original Norse spelling of the name, *Rognvaldsvao*, the *vao* would have referred to the tarbet across the neck of Langness which was used as the pathway when the Viking longboats were dragged over to the other side of the peninsula and the quieter waters of Castletown Bay. Ronaldsway is also reputed to be the site of King Orry's castle and it has been the scene of many a battle. After the execution of *Illiam Dhone,* his estate of Ronaldsway was sequestrated but later returned to his family, and the last man to include Ronaldsway in his title was a direct descendant of William Christian, Rear-Admiral Sir Hugh Christian who was elevated to the peerage but who died just before the patent reached him.

Public Amenities
Ballasalla Post Office (0624) 822531
Malew Parish Commissioners (Town Hall)
 (0624) 823522
Police Station (not continuously manned)
 (0624) 822543, (0624) 631212
Banks
Isle of Man Bank, Station Road (0624) 822503
Leisure Centre
Silverdale Glen Cafe (0624) 823474

DERBYHAVEN

Heading out beyond the airport perimeter the car driver can easily find the way to the picturesque hamlet of Derbyhaven. There is an occasional bus service to this part of the Island but the casual traveller is advised to check with the bus company (Manx National Transport). Well utilised by small boats, it no longer has any commercial shipping activities, but at the time of the Vikings and their medieval successors, it was a thriving port.

The old Smelthouse at Derbyhaven, whose remains are still visible, probably dates from around 1711. It was here that Blacksmith John Wilks – two former Governors of the Bank of England are directly descended from him – made the Island's first penny coins, an action which Tynwald vindicated by making them legal tender. There is solid evidence to prove that exclusively Manx coinage was minted by one John Murrey a merchant of Douglas in 1668 and he appears to have been the owner of the Derbyhaven Mint. Incidentally, it seems that the rate of exchange decided upon in 1709 by James II, tenth Earl of Derby, when he authorised a new issue was fourteen Manx pennies to twelve British, but by the time the only Manx money issued under Atholl rule came on the market, the rate of exchange was only half, and that in favour of the British coinage.

The sandy turf of the Langness Peninsula is home to the famous Castletown Golf Links. There cannot be many hotels where you can step out of the front door onto the first tee and play on a world class golf course. The Castletown Golf Links Hotel with its excellent facilities offers an ideal opportunity to take a break and get away from it all.

Close by the ruins of the Smelthouse is the 10th hole and it was here 153 years before it was transferred to Epsom Downs in 1780 that the famous Derby horse race originated. It seems that the seventh Earl of Derby wished to encourage the breeding of Manx horses and as an incentive presented a cup to be won in open competition. One stipulation he did put on the race was that only those horses that had been foaled within the Island or the Calf of Man were allowed to be entered. The Manx horses of that period were small and very hardy, renowned for their speed, surefootedness and stamina. It may well be that prior to the Derby the only time horses were in competition was after a wedding when the guests raced back to the bridegrooms home to claim the honour of breaking the bride-cake over the bride's head, as she entered her new home!

Langness is very well known for its wildlife and by far the best way to view it is to walk. There is a variety of bird life and on a pleasant summer's

Derbyhaven

evening nothing can be better than to watch the seals swimming about or just taking life easy at Dreswick Point, the southern-most tip of the Isle of Man. Please do not be misled by the sometimes peaceful waters, they conceal jagged rocks which have claimed many lives. A short distance from the lighthouse and in line with the Herring Tower is Tharastack Gulley, where in 1853 the crew of the Plymouth schooner "Provider" perished. These poor souls were buried in sight of the wreck and their burial-place is marked by a natural tombstone of rock carved with the vessel's name and the date of her loss.

CASTLETOWN

Distances Ballasalla 3m, Douglas 9m, Laxey 20m, Peel 13m, Ramsey 26m, Port Erin 5m, Port St Mary 7m.

The ancient Capital of Mann for several centuries, Castletown has a charm all of its own. Sited at the edge of a long extinct and almost untraceable volcano, the town was guardian for the Manx in times of war and peace. The virtual end to commercial seaborne traffic came in the 1970's but in more recent times there has been a revival in business, with a number of commercial activities based on the finance sector being located there. It is the only town in the parish of Malew and as a result of long association with the seat of government, visitors to the area will soon pick out many anglicised names around the town and its vicinity. Names to look out for are Bowling Green, Great Meadow, Paradise (now Ellerslie and the former home of General Cuming who was with Wolfe at Quebec), Red Gap, Witches Mill and the Rope Walk. Many of the homestead names in the proximity such as *Grenaby, Tosaby* and *Orrisdale* testify to the fact that Castletown and its surrounding area were well colonised by the Norsemen.

Journeying to Castletown is made easy by the regularity of the bus service and the steam railway which operates in both directions several times a day during the summer. Well signposted roads offer alternative approaches to the town. The narrow streets of Castletown evoke memories of yesteryear and a pleasant time can be had by merely strolling around the town, but with so much else to see it deserves a long visit.

Finishing its journey from the highlands of the parish the Silverburn gently empties into the picturesque harbour, pausing, almost as if for a last

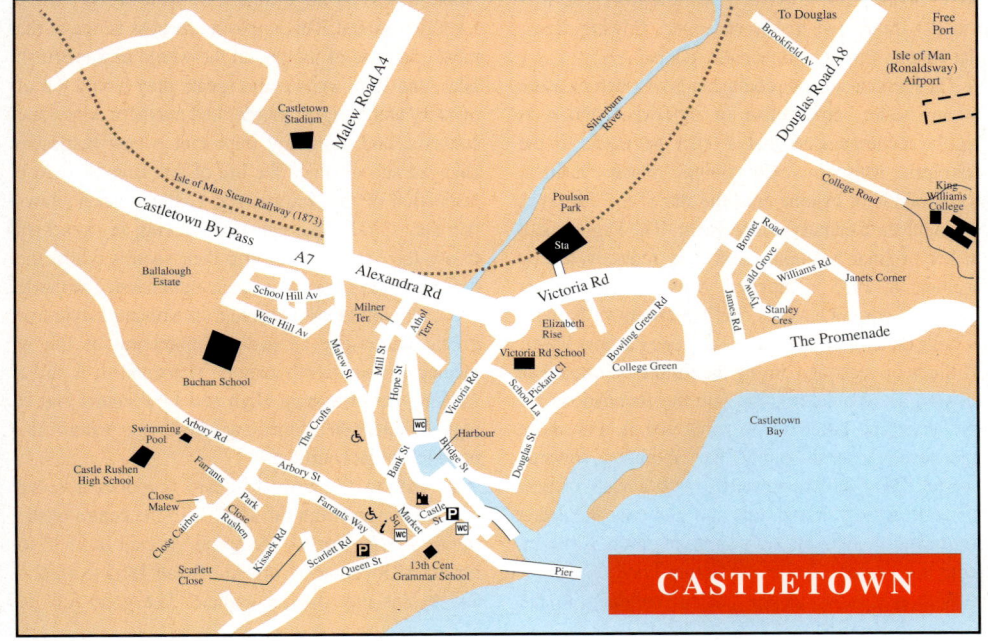

Castletown – Castle Rushen

look around, as it flows under the Apostles Bridge. It's easy to work out where the bridge gets the name from! There is one other river in the area, which makes its entry into the sea just on the western edge of the town at Red Gap. It rejoices in the unusual name of the "Dumb River", so called because it is literally dumb and makes no sound, flowing across flat country throughout its entire course.

The harbour without doubt can give much pleasure to any sailor, prospective or otherwise, and it is highly recommended that a visit be made to the Nautical Museum. Containing much nautical memorabilia of bygone eras, the star of the display is the eighteenth century armed yacht "The Peggy", still in her original boathouse and only rediscovered by accident in 1935, a hundred years after her owner Captain George Quayle's death. Castletown harbour is built on a shelf of lava, clearly seen at low water. Millions of years ago during the formation of the Isle of Man a volcanic eruption laid the foundations for the landscape much as we now see it. For those interested, a stroll along the shoreline towards Scarlett Point will be rewarded with a view of past volcanic activity. Wind, tide and rain over the aeons have exposed the volcano's surviving plug. Close by there is a Visitors Centre and Nature Trail.

With practically all the ancient buildings in the town grouped around the harbour and to the seaward side of the Castle, there is a virtual treasure trove for the serious historian and casual visitor alike. There is for instance the old Castletown Grammar School, built originally as the ancient capital's first church in approximately 1200; it played an important part in later centuries in the education of the young people of the Island. Nearby is the old garrison church of St. Mary's built in 1826 to replace Bishop Wilson's church of 1698, saved in recent times from dereliction and now a thriving business house. In 1777 John Wesley, the founder of Methodism paying his first visit to the Island, preached in front of the Castle and noted in his journal of the 30th June, that "A more loving, simple-hearted people than this I never saw".

A walk up from the outer harbour through the narrow streets will bring you to the old House of Keys building, which for a long time, from 1709, was the seat of government until population and commercial pressures forced the Keys to decamp to Douglas in 1869. The builder's receipt shows that the building was constructed for the princely sum of £83-5s-6½d.

Standing sentinel over Castletown and the southern lowlands is Castle Rushen. Dating from Norse times, its huge limestone structure is visible for miles around. This imposing fortress is one of the most complete of its type in the whole of the British Isles, and if its walls could speak, they would tell of mystery and intrigue, murder and mayhem, kings and consorts, and the many important events that have changed and moulded the life of this Island. A close inspection of the staircases at Castle Rushen shows that they spiral to the right, thus forcing any attackers to use their left hand to grip their swords whilst the defenders were free to use their right hand. The castle is a living building, decorated in authentic style and giving the visitor an instant impression of life in medieval/ seventeenth century Manxland. It is still a working castle hosting High and Low courts and at regular intervals witnessing weddings within the precincts of its courthouse.

A visit to the market square produces a scene hardly changed from the 1800's. In the centre of the square stands Smelt's Memorial, erected in 1838 to honour a Governor – Cornelius Smelt 1805 to 1832 – and to this day still incomplete. The good folk of

Castletown refused to contribute for a statue to grace the column and for the first few years after it was erected it became known as the "Castletown Candlestick". Today it gives sterling service as a traffic roundabout... have a look at the plaque on the side, you will find it interesting. Across the way from the Smelt Memorial is the former home of Captain John Quilliam RN who fought at the Battle of Trafalgar and saved HMS "Victory" from destruction by rigging a jury (temporary) rudder at the height of the fighting. Looking down on the square is a clock presented to the Island by Queen Elizabeth I. It has only ever had one finger and is still going strong after almost four hundred years.

The outskirts of Castletown have had almost as much history as the town itself. Lying to the East of the old metropolis is King William's College, a long time centre of public school education, its great central tower dominating the landscape. The idea of the College probably first surfaced in a letter from the seventh Earl of Derby, *Yn Stanlagh Mooar*, in a letter to his son Charles but due to the subsequent outbreak of the English Civil War, his idea did not come to fruition until 1833. Facing the school is Hango Hill, where *Illiam Dhone* met his end. The Norse name for the hill was *Hangaholl*, or Hill of Hanging, and William Christian was the last person to be executed there. It is also a very important archaeological site. The ruins are in fact of a blockhouse built by the seventh Earl at the time of the unrest in England.

To the West of the town is the Balladoole estate centred on the fine Balladoole House, the home of the Stevensons for many hundreds of years. There is evidence in the Manx Museum that at least six generations of the family lived on the estate prior to a mention in the manorial records of 1511. John Stevenson was the Speaker of the House of Keys, 1704 to 1738 and his name should forever be remembered by the Manx Nation for the manner in which he led the Keys in their patriotic struggle against the tenth Earl of Derby. Bishop Wilson called him "The Father of his Country" and at one time he was imprisoned in Castle Rushen for championing the rights of his fellow countrymen. The last bearer of the family name was Sir Ralph Stevenson, who retired as British Ambassador to Egypt in 1955 and

Castletown – Harbour

who suffered great agonies as the British, French and Israelis stormed ashore at the time Nasser appropriated the Suez Canal just a year later.

To the West of Balladoole is *Poyll Vaaish,* which is easily reached by car or on foot from Castletown by following the coastal footpath *Raad ny Foillan,* The Road of the Gull. The walk from Castletown hosts marvellous views of the surrounding countryside. A particular favourite of the locals is the panoramic vista looking northwards as the low hills of the coastal areas roll ever upwards to the central mountain range, with *Snaefell* visible in the far distance. Just after dropping down from the basaltic Stack of Scarlett the walker comes upon a small quarry which produces high quality black marble. It was from this source that Bishop Wilson gifted the stone from which the steps of St. Paul's Cathedral were made, and again in recent years replaced when worn out. Close by the Stevenson's ancestral home there is the site of a Viking Ship burial mound and this together with a number of important archaeological sites makes a visit to the area well worthwhile.

At the point where the coastal footpath joins the main road (A5) is the area known as *Poyll Vaaish* or translated into the English "Death Pool or Bay of Death". Probably the name is derived from the black marble which comprises the sea bed in the vicinity and the ripples of lava clearly seen above the low water mark. There are legends galore about this corner of the Island. Stories of shipwrecks, pirates, and looters abound, and on a wet and windy night it is not too difficult to imagine the calls of distressed sailors wafting shoreward on the breeze.

Strandhall which lies to the right when heading on South has a spring flowing down onto the shore and legend tells that, although the source of the spring lies many feet above sea level, it is reputed to be a salt water spring with petrifying powers. Indeed at extremely low tides and particularly after a storm has moved the sands, the remains of a large petrified forest can sometimes be seen.

Rounding *Baie ny Carrickey,* The Bay of the Rocks, the road follows the water's edge passing as it does the Treen lands of *Kentraugh,* "Shore End", the home of the Gawne family for centuries. There are fine sands here with excellent boating waters but as ever please watch the weather and tides, the sea can play strange tricks on the unsuspecting. At the West end of the bay lies *Gansey,* this Scandinavian name means Magic Bay. Peaceful now but in the past, the scene of many a struggle between the forces of law and order and the farmers and fishermen of Mann. It is interesting to note that in the short distance between Castletown and *Kentraugh* the traveller has moved across three parishes, Malew, Arbory and into Rushen.

Public Amenities

Castletown Post Office (0624) 822516
Castletown Commissioners (Town Hall)
  (0624) 825005
Harbour Master's Office (0624) 823549
Police Station (not continuously manned)
  (0624) 822222, (0624) 631212

Banks

Barclays, Market Square (Central Switchboard)
  (0624) 682000
Isle of Man Bank, Market Square (0624) 822503
TSB Bank, Market Square (0624) 822755

Leisure Centre

Southern Swimming Pool, Arbory Road
  (0624) 823930

Tourist Information

Castle Rushen (0624) 823326
Castletown Station (Seasonal) (0624) 822275

LOW COST TRAVEL SPECIALISTS

FOR INCLUSIVE packages to the ISLE OF MAN
CALL US NOW ON:

0345 581407

and ask for your free 'HERITAGE ISLE' Brochure.
Special Railway weeks and events organised

ATOL
1965

A FULLY BONDED COMPANY

ABTA
A7496

PORT ST MARY

Distances Ballasalla 7m, Castletown 4m, Douglas 16m, Laxey 24m, Peel 16m, Port Erin 2m, Ramsey 28m.

Ahead of you lies the pretty fishing village of Port St. Mary, which is the English form of the Gaelic *Keeill Moirrey,* more commonly referred to as *Purt-le-Moirrey.* The impressive backdrop to this village is the Mull Peninsula with its steep slopes and fields rolling right down into the village itself. Part of the land has been turned into a fine 9-hole golf course which is popular with locals and visitors alike.

At one time a thriving fishing port, home for both local and Scottish vessels, it is now full of fine yachts and leisure vessels of all types.

The breakwater gives good shelter and its deepwater berths prove popular with visiting sailors and the few remaining fishing vessels. The inner pier, the Alfred Pier, named after a previous Duke of Edinburgh who laid the foundation stone in 1882, shelters the smaller craft and is a very picturesque part of the Port. Clustered round the harbour are old Manx cottages – thatched roofs having long ago given way to Manx slate – transporting the visitor back in time to a more relaxed way of life. The newer part of Port St. Mary lies above the sandy beach of Chapel Bay where generations of children have learned to swim and to build their first sandcastles. Linking the harbour and the bay is a fine walkway winding its way close to the water's edge. The local pubs once frequented solely by the men of the fishing fleet, now garner their harvest from the yachting fraternity and the passing tourist trade.

Perwick, owes its name to the old Scandinavian word for Harbour Creek. In very recent times the hotel that once stood at the edge of the cliff has been developed for private housing but the beach is still worth a visit, particularly if you have more than a passing interest in geology. There is a very noticeable "fault" on the South East side of Perwick Bay which clearly shows where the carboniferous and slate rocks meet under an overlay of glacial clay. Until the beginning of this century there were the remains of a fort to be seen on the shore. Now the best play area for the young ones is the rocky pools and small caves at the foot of the cliffs.

PORT ST. MARY AND PORT ERIN

Port St. Mary

Climbing out of the Port, the next village is Fistard which sits high on the hillside above Perwick Bay. Fistard gives its name to the Treen which includes Port St Mary and is the Scandinavian for Fish's Garth or Farm. Perhaps it is the fact that the village and its near neighbour the Howe are perched high above the world below that accounts for the timelessness of the area. Little seems to have changed as the years roll by and even though the villagers often earn their living elsewhere, the hustle and bustle of modern life is left behind at the foot of the hill. The student of history researching the OS maps of last century will see that the Howe has slightly changed position. The Howe is one of the few English place names on the Isle of Man and is probably from the meaning of hill. So as not to offend the good neighbours of the Howe, we had better leave the village where it is!

Public Amenities

Harbour Master's Office (0624) 833206
Police Station (not continuously manned)
 (0624) 833222, (0624) 631212
Port St Mary Commissioners (Town Hall)
 (0624) 832101
Port St Mary Post Office (0624) 833113

CREGNEASH

Leaving the narrow lanes of Fistard and the Howe behind, the A31 climbs still higher up Mull Hill to the village of *Cregneash*. Don't worry if your map refers to it as *Cregneish*, the first spelling is the Gaelic way. It means Rock of Ages. The village is the oldest in the Isle of Man and part of it forms the Folk Museum run by Manx National Heritage. The thatched cottages nestle in and around a sleepy hollow and the views of the Calf of Man and the Sound are stunning. If you like agriculture, the Museum's working farm is a must and you may also be lucky and see the thatcher at work. As with the two lower villages, the people of the Mull Peninsula cling to old-time customs and have been little influenced by the march of progress.

Across the way from the "modern" village lies the remains of an older village. The Mull Circle, in Manx *Meayl*, meaning Bald or Bare Hill, dates back to the late Neolithic or early Bronze Age. Used primarily as a prehistoric burial place, it is unique in archaeology terms, combining the circle form with six pairs of cists, each pair having a passage between which radiates outwards. The prehistoric village was below the circle and hut foundations and other relics were discovered on the site. In case you think the Martians have landed nearby, they haven't! What you are actually seeing on the hilltop above the village is a Radiobeacon that just happens to look like a flying saucer... from a distance! Trans Atlantic flights home in on this beacon when making their landfall from the new world. The huddle of buildings nearby house a similar system for Irish Sea shipping. A walk on past the beacons brings you to the Spanish Head Manx National Trust area, home to the incredible Chasms – described more fully in the Cliffs section of the Guide.

If you missed a snack at Cregneash, don't worry, just carry on down the hill, and Terry Jackson and his team will ensure that you are well fed and watered at the Sound Cafe, where they generate their own wind powered electricity. The culinary delights of this cafe have a reputation second to none for home made meals and snacks. Give yourself plenty of time here as it is a number one beauty spot. The Sound – the

FALCON'S NEST HOTEL LIMITED

The family run hotel that caters for your sheer pleasure..
Enjoy the A la Carte Restaurants, a simple bar lunch or Sunday Carvery.
Whether on holiday or business savour the excellent cuisine and the magnificent scenery.
Open all year round and only 10 minutes from the airport.
REAL ALES, FOOD & REAL ATMOSPHERE
*Falcon's Nest Hotel
Port Erin, Isle of Man
Tel: (0624) 834077
Fax: (0624) 835370*
BOOKINGS BY FAX OR PHONE

Land's End of Mann – is a good place to stretch stiff limbs or as a starting off point for more energetic exercise. Try the walk back to Port St Mary or on to Port Erin, it is well worth it.

PORT ERIN

Distances Ballasalla 6m, Castletown 5m, Douglas 15m, Laxey 23m, Peel 16m, Port St Mary 2m, Ramsey 28m.

Whichever way you approach Port Erin, be it from the North, South, East or by sea from the West there is one common denominator, the views are impressive. Port Erin translated means either Lord's Port or Iron Port and in the Manx Gaelic it is written as *Purt Chiarn.* Latter day smugglers came to know Port Erin very well, using the solitude of the bay to mask their activities and kept save from observation by the steep hills and perpendicular cliffs surrounding the village. In modern times the village became the playground of the Lancashire mill owners and their employees, and it is no wonder the peace and contentment that the visitors of the early part of the twentieth century experienced could well be described as "far from the madding crowd".

That description still applies and the Port Erin Group of Hotels certainly adhere to the principle of a healthy visitor making for a happy holiday maker. With five of their hotels to choose from there should be little difficulty in picking a package to suit your own specific tastes. Founded by the late Jack Wilson, the Group appreciates that the holiday-maker after a refreshing day out in the countryside may not feel like going too far afield after a huge Manx dinner, so Port Erin Hotels bring the evening's entertainment to you. Recognising that today's tourist is an experienced traveller who is no longer content with the old style of seaside boarding house or an impersonal modern concrete box, the team at Port Erin Hotels concentrate on prime considerations such as the comforts of home, good food, friendly "natives" and above all no hassle.

One of the newest hotel developments in recent years has been the Cherry Orchard Hotel. The vision shown in the building of this combined hotel and self-catering apartments complex, is recognised far and wide as a step into the future for the Island. The success of the development is in its ability to produce high value, low cost holidays. The facilities available at this family run AA and RAC 3 Star Hotel ensure that whatever your age, you can relax and enjoy modern in-house leisure facilities and savour the

Port Erin from the Ballnahowe Road

Port Erin – Railway Station

excellent cuisine. If Port Erin suits your fancy, then a call to the Cherry Orchard's holiday department will allow you to take advantage of their special travel inclusive packages.

Situated at the head of an almost landlocked bay, guarded to the North by lofty Bradda Head and the Castle Rocks and Mull Peninsula to the South, Port Erin offers a sheltered play area in most weathers. Pretty white painted cottages trim the inner edge of the bay, bordered by grassy banks, rising up to a more formal promenade fronting a traditional line of seaside hotels. As with all seaside towns there are a variety of places to eat and drink. When you spot the Okell's sign you can usually sort out lunch or snack requirements. Port Erin is a very photogenic place by virtue of its symmetry with sea, sand, cliffs, hill and heather. Stir into that combination, shadows and brilliant sunsets often framed by the Mountains of Mourne, and you have a picture painted by God's own hand. If you have left your sketch book at home, don't worry! Rosemary and her staff at the Bridge Bookshop can supply most forms of art equipment, just in case the mood to sketch or paint creeps up on you. Holidays are usually the only time most busy people have to catch up on their reading and they also have a good selection of books to choose from. If you would like some culture whilst on holiday, check with the Erin Arts Centre, they frequently hold musical and artistic events.

Over one hundred years ago the excellence of the waters offshore from Port Erin was recognised and the Marine Biological Station was established at the seaward end of the bay. Still operating, now as an annex to Liverpool University, it is well known and respected throughout the marine world. Many famous experts consult the Station and no less a personage than the late Emperor of Japan, a renowned marine life specialist, frequently made contact – a tradition maintained by the present Emperor who has in fact visited in person. Directly opposite this seat of learning are the remains of a breakwater started in 1864 and meant to turn the bay into the national harbour of refuge. William Milner of Bradda Head fame was a staunch supporter of the breakwater and he along with everyone else on the Island would have felt a great sense of loss when in one single night in January 1884, it was destroyed in a storm.

One of the more famous residents of Port Erin in

THE CHERRY ORCHARD HOTEL

AA ★★★ RAC ★★★
COMMENDED

Situated in the South of the Island, with its rugged cliffs and magnificent seascapes, The Cherry Orchard Holiday complex provides a wide choice of holiday accommodation to suit all pockets. You can choose between well appointed en-suite rooms or fully maintained self catering apartments which are free of any utility charges.

The facilities available in this family run AA and RAC 3 star Hotel and Self-catering Apartments ensure that whatever your age, you can relax, enjoy modern in-house leisure facilities and savour excellent cuisine in the restaurant.

The Cherry Orchard is an ideal base from which to discover all the Island's attractions and amenities, including 3 Golf Courses, all within easy reach of the Hotel complex.

Port Erin with its village atmosphere, sandy beaches and sheltered bay provides the ideal location for those who enjoy sea sports, walking and bird-watching.

FIND OUT MORE ABOUT OUR HIGH VALUE LOW COST HOLIDAYS INCLUDING SPECIAL RATES FOR CHILDREN.

The Cherry Orchard, Bridson Street, Port Erin, Isle of Man
Telephone 0624 833511 • Fax 0624 833583
FOR FURTHER DETAILS FREEPHONE 0800 833627

recent years has been World Champion Formula 1 and Indianapolis Champion, Nigel Mansell. Nigel loves the unhurried way of life on the Island and particularly in Port Erin. He always got great pleasure from the fine golf course. A son of Port Erin who made his way to the far side of the earth seeking fame and fortune was William Kermode, born in 1775. Taking up a grant of land in Van Diemen's Land, now of course known as Tasmania, he amassed a fortune and contributed valuable service to the Tasmanian Legislative Council. A story from that far off land tells of how Kermode was ambushed in his coach by two bush rangers who demanded his money or his life. Reacting faster than the robbers, he smacked their heads together, bound them up and drove to Hobart where the law recognised them as the most dangerous men of the day. Robert Quayle Kermode, the son, also did sterling work in Tasmania having a large say in the abolition of the Australian State's convict status.

Public Amenities
Harbour Master's Office (0624) 833205
Police Station (not continuously manned)
    (0624) 832222, (0624) 631212
Port Erin Commissioners Office (Town Hall)
    (0624) 832298
Port Erin Post Office (0624) 833119

Banks
Barclays, Station Road (Central Switchboard)
    (0624) 682000
Isle of Man Bank, Station Road (0624) 833120

Tourist Information
Port Erin Bus Depot (0624) 833125
Port Erin Railway Station (Seasonal) (0624) 833432

BRIDGE BOOKSHOP
Shore Road, Port Erin
(0624) 833376
Wide selection of books. We also sell Art material, Music, Videos, CD's and Cassettes
Extended hours during Summer

The Island's favourite brewery

Proud to comply with the Manx Pure Beer Act of 1874

Producers of a wide range of superb cask conditioned ales

An authentic cold-conditioned continental style pilsner beer

Numerous bottled beers and celebration brews

Available Island-wide & throughout the U.K.

For details of how to obtain our hand crafted beers, (wholesale or retail) souvenir merchandising, or arrange a tour of the brewery, telephone Ian Caines or Martin Brunnschweiler on 0624 661244

Port Erin Beach

COLBY AND BALLABEG

To the East of Port Erin in the flat lands of Arbory are the villages of Colby and Ballabeg. *Colby,* Kolli's Farm, stands at the entrance to the delightful Colby Glen. A walk up the Glen takes the visitor alongside a babbling brook as it runs its lower course through wooded glades and higher still where the gorse is a riot of colour. Further up the Glen there are the remains of *Keeill Catreeney* and a burial ground. The ancient St Catherine's or Colby Fair used to be held here. Nearby there is *Chibbyrt Catreeney,* Catherine's Well, and it was woe betide anyone who slated their thirst from the well, as they were afflicted with an unquenchable thirst for ever. Incidentally, if you are thirsty, the Colby Glen Hotel is nearby and will look after your needs more than adequately, and you can have a very nice meal there.

Another fair, which has survived to this very day is *Laa Columb Killey,* St Columba's Day Fair. Held in a special field in either Colby or Ballabeg at the end of June each year, it attracts people from all over the Island and gives a glimpse of country life as it used to be. *Ballabeg* is on the ancient quarterland and the village is named from the 1511 Manorial Roll as Begson's Farm. The area is very much rural and the quiet sheltered lanes are lined by foxgloves and wild fuschia. If you are in a vehicle, pull over and park, enjoy what the ramblers hear... the occasional bleat of a sheep or the song of a bird, the rustle of the ferns and grasses as the breezes keep them moving in a fan like action. Weedkillers and pesticides are not used on the Manx hedgerows and it is still possible to see wild flowers which have disappeared from other parts of the British Isles due to irresponsible husbandry of the countryside. The lanes of Arbory and the neighbouring parishes of Malew and Rushen play host to a multitude of plant and animal life.

The church has always played an important part in the life of the South of the Island and none more so than Kirk Arbory. Built in 1757 the present church has an oak beam supporting the roof which belonged to two previous churches. There is an inscription on the beam mentioning Thomas Radcliffe, Abbot of Rushen and it seems to refer to the Stanley crest of an Eagle and Child. The grave of Captain Quilliam of H.M.S. "Victory" and Trafalgar fame is in the churchyard. Along the road from the church towards Castletown is Friary Farm. Clearly visible from the road are the remains of the Friary of Bemaken, founded by the Grey Friars in 1373. The holy men were assisted in its completion by stone masons who were on the Island to do work on Castle Rushen. Employed by William de Montacute and later his son, the masons were on the move around Britain strengthening castles and fortifications between 1368 and 1374. Two Ogham stones were found on the site and are now in the safe keeping of the Manx Museum. The stones are inscribed in the ancient British and Irish alphabet Ogham which was used for writing Irish from the fourth or fifth century A.D. to the early seventh century.

GLEN MAYE, DALBY, AND NIARBYL

Glion Muigh, Yellow Glen, is a village sitting on steep hillsides at the bottom end of the mining glens of Glen Mooar and Glen Rushen. On beyond the village the river plunges over a series of waterfalls, before finishing its dash to the sea between two hundred foot high, gorse and heather clad cliffs. It is easy to see that the village of Glen Maye owes its existence to the farming and mining industries and the good efforts of the householders have ensured that it has retained its old character. A favourite watering hole for locals, and the tourists who discover it, is the Waterfall Hotel. On a fine summer's eve a pleasant hour or two can be whiled away in the Inn and the beautiful glen offers a delightful opportunity to walk your lunch or evening meal off.

Niarbyl, or to give it its Manx name *Yn Arbyl,* The Tail, on account of the long reef jutting out from the shoreline, is an ideal place for picnics; the superb views to the North and South still thrill, no matter how many times you see it. The isolation of this part of the Island can best be seen from here. The full grandeur of the south western coast can clearly be contemplated, with the massive cliffs stretching away southward in a series of giant headlands and bays before Bradda Head interrupts the flow briefly. The Mull Hills continue the vista and from this angle it almost seems as if the Calf of Man is joined to the main island. Wonderful country for walking, it is not necessary to travel in and out of the area to enjoy it. The Ballacallin Hotel at Dalby has a great reputation for food, and Joe and Lindsay give a warm welcome to all, particularly ramblers. Modern en-suite accommodation allows you to put your weary feet up and relax whilst planning the next day's walk.

FOXDALE

Foxdale means Waterfall Dale and with the area containing many streams, it is aptly named. Once upon a time it was a famous centre for lead mining and from the three hundred or so tons of ore that were mined each month, some fifteen to twenty ounces of silver per ton were extracted. Closed down for good in the early part of the century, many of the miners emigrated to the colonies, and it has taken years for the village to begin to recover some of its lost prosperity. Times are improving and the economic life of Foxdale is slowly returning the area to its former glory. By the way, if you are a keen fisherman call in and see Bill Duquemin at The Tackle Box, he is a "mine" of information on fishing.

Ballacallin Country Pub & Hotel
Dalby
Tel: 842030

Comfortable, modern en-suite accommodation with TV/Tea & Coffee-making facilities
Please send for our brochure
Spectacular Sunsets and Western Coastal Views
Lunchtime and Evening Meals served every day. Morning Coffees and Afternoon Teas
Traditional Sunday Lunch and Bar Meals served on Sundays between 12 noon & 3pm
Personally supervised by Joe and Lindsay
Live Entertainment on certain evenings
SUN TERRACE   CHILDREN WELCOME
"Highly recommended" in Camra Good Beer Guide for excellent beer and quality catering

---

View from Kerroodhoo

Bill's refreshing style of customer relations assures a welcome to all. Even if you are not a fishing type he is a helpful guide on all manner of subjects. Not content with an Island horizon, he has a thriving worldwide export business.

Many of the farms in the area are branching out into tourism, by converting outbuildings and old cottages to self-catering use. One such farm, *Kionslieu*, standing on the hillside above Foxdale is a fine example of a conversion. Guests live in close contact with the daily routine of a working farm and if the children like animals then their stay will be

Niarbyl

idyllic. *Kionslieu* has an ideal name for its situation, but there are no prizes for guessing! The rural location belies the fact that the main towns and beauty spots are only a few minutes drive from the farm and in the evening if you feel like a good pint or glass of cheer, the Baltic is only a short walk away.

Kionslieu Farm, Higher Foxdale.
Telephone: 0624 801349

Kionslieu Farm Cottages are a combination of newly-built and renovated farm buildings set in the peaceful Foxdale countryside. These spacious, centrally-heated cottages are fully-equipped, right down to the linen and towels. The traditional yard with friendly farm animals and delightful rural views make Kionslieu Farm Cottages an idyllic holiday home.

You will be a mere ten minutes walk from the village shop and inn, and just ten minutes drive from Douglas, Castletown and Peel.

EXPECTED GRADING 4 KEYS
HIGHLY COMMENDED

PEEL

Distances Ballasalla 10m, Castletown 13m, Douglas 11m, Laxey 19m, Port Erin 16m, Port St Mary 16m, Ramsey 16m.

Peel has to be to the fore-front in everyone's touring plans of the Island. Taking its name from the castle, the name appears in the 1231 Papal Bull of Gregory IX as *Pile*, which was an alternative name for *Inis Patrick*, St Patrick's Isle. Peel, in its abbreviated form, only came into everyday use in the nineteenth century, although it was being used at the beginning of the eighteenth century. The Gaelic for the city is *Purt ny Hinshey*, Island Town. Always a centre of civilisation, Peel is so steeped in history that to attempt to do more than give a flavour of the place would be to commit an injustice. Do give time, plenty of it in your programme to take in the sights and atmosphere of this ancient city for that is what it is, being the proud possessor of a Cathedral down through the centuries. The present Pro-Cathedral in the centre of Peel is a fine building, well worth a visit.

There have been numerous periods of importance in Peel's history, many of which have played a roll in the development of the Island's nation-hood. The Viking settlement of the area was one such occasion and excavations have uncovered important burial sites. One site revealed the remains of a female subsequently known as "The Pagan Lady". The grave was unusual in that it was a curious mixture of Christian and Pagan rituals. A very fine bead necklace was recovered from the grave and you can see the real thing in the Museum at Douglas.

Very important prisoners have been incarcerated in Peel Castle over the ages and the Bard himself, William Shakespeare, makes mention in Henry VI of one famous detainee, Eleanor – Duchess of Gloucester. For fourteen long and difficult years the Cathedral crypt was the prison of the Duchess, who was accused of treason and sorcery against Henry VI as she sought to advance her husband's claim to the throne of England. Her fellow plotters were not to taste the "joys" of Manx prison life as Roger Bolingbroke was executed and Margery Joudemain, the Witch of Eye, was burnt to death. History records

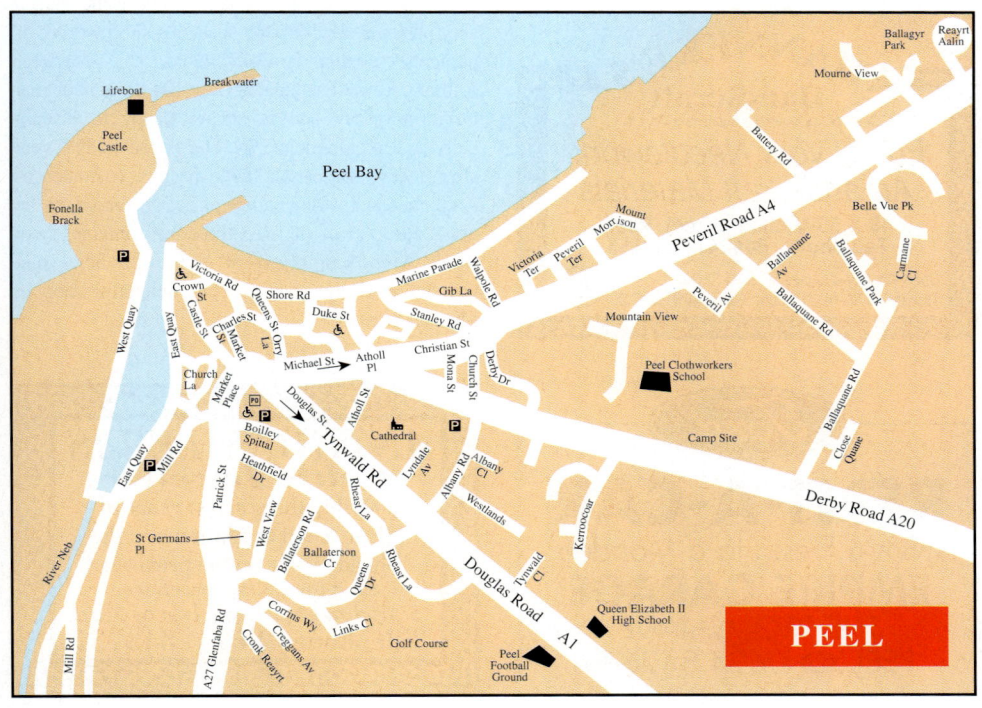

Come West to
PEEL BOOKS
for
- A wide range of Books, including Manx interest
- Maps, guides, yachting charts
- Spoken-word cassettes
- Children's reading and activity books
- Fine Art and Woven Silk Cards

and a warm welcome

Pram and wheelchair access
Atholl Place, Peel.
Telephone: 0624 843738

HANNEKE'S Handicraft
(The Mansk-Svenska Publishing Co. Ltd.)

For all your Needlework, Art and Craft Materials

48 & 50 Michael Street, Peel.
Telephone: 844241 / 842855

Open Monday–Wednesday 9.30-17.00
Thursday 9.30-14.00 Friday–Saturday 9.30-17.00

that she was a difficult prisoner, who had to be carefully guarded against escape or even suicide. If such a wealthy and perhaps arrogant woman could be held against her will in conditions of great deprivation, it is not a wonder that her ghost is said to haunt the crypt.

Once bitten by the Peel bug, most people park their vehicles and walk everywhere, but just in case you are visiting or staying here and are without transport, the aptly named Empire Garage can take care of your transport requirements. No problem in finding them, just wander along the Promenade taking in the august, almost imperial looking coastline extending away northwards. The amiable staff will soon fix you up with a suitable car to extend your island exploration.

The narrow streets of Peel with their sandstone built cottages and houses act as a wonderful backdrop to the bay. Many of the buildings have changed use from their original purpose and it is a fascinating way of enjoying a walk around the city by guessing the former use of the old buildings. The shops offer a variety of goods and although lacking any of the big national superstores, they do give a very personal service. One specialist shop worthy of particular mention is Celtic Gold. The proprietor Anthony Lewis has created over 300 designs of fine Celtic jewellery and is always happy to discuss individual requirements. If "The Pagan Lady" were alive today, she would have been a customer of Anthony's and with a choice of designs based on the rich Celtic Art of the past three millenniums, there would have been plenty of choice for her. Treat yourself and pay a visit to this delightful shop in Michael Street.

Ford
RENT-A-CAR
from a Fiesta to a Mondeo
EMPIRE GARAGE
THE PROMENADE
PEEL ☎ 0624 842666

ANTHONY LEWIS
Celtic Jeweller
Possibly the greatest range of Silver, Gold & Platinum in the World. Made on the premises.
Send for Colour brochure.
5 Michael St, Peel, Isle of Man
Telephone: (0624) 843737

Peel Harbour

Peel Seafront

Education has always been valued by the people of the West and Philip Christian, a native born son of the city who died in 1655, left money to educate the poorest boys and girls of Peel. Moving towards more modern times there have been Latin, Navigation, English and Mathematical schools in Peel and there is now a very fine High School, opened only a few years ago by Her Majesty the Queen, in whose honour it is named. The habit of savouring the written word still strongly exists over in the far side of the Island and Peel Books in Atholl Place can supply the visitor with a wide variety of books and artistic goods. If you happen to be a visiting yachtsman, call in and see the good folk here, they can take care of your chart requirements. Hobbies are catered for in Michael Street, where Hanneke's Handicrafts are able to fulfil your needlework requirements. If your forte is painting then the friendly Dutch lady can advise you on painting eggs right through the spectrum to glass painting, and she operates a mail order service.

One of Peel's greatest exports has been its people and with a strong tradition of seamanship behind them, it is small wonder that the sons and daughters of what must be the smallest city in the British Isles have spread out all over the world. George Cannon was born in Michael Street on the 3rd December 1794. Some thirty one years later he married Ann Quayle, a girl from round the corner in Douglas Street. After becoming converts to the Mormon faith, they emigrated along with thousands of others to the USA. Departing from Liverpool on 3rd September 1842 on the sailing ship "Sydney", the voyage was to be one of tragedy for the family as, forty one days out, the cold waters of the Atlantic received the body of Ann Quayle. Two years after leaving Liverpool to seek religious freedom, both parents had died but their memory lives on in the hearts of some twenty thousand direct descendants, many of them leaders in their own fields of work becoming Congressmen, Senators, Chief Justices, Federal Judges and much more. On your walk round Peel have a look at number 25 Douglas Street... that's where Ann Quayle lived.

Obviously during the course of your wanderings the pangs of thirst and hunger may well strike. Peel has a variety of pubs, hotels, snack bars and cafes, each reflecting their own style. Sport is important in Peel and besides the Kart racing there are occasions when sand racing attracts thousands of people to the seafront. Golf is popular and the eighteen hole course presents a real challenge

Public Amenities
Harbour Master's Office (0624) 842338
Peel Commissioners (Town Hall) (0624) 842341
Peel Post Office (0624) 842282
Police Station (not continuously manned)
 (0624) 842208, (0624) 631212
Banks
Barclays, Michael Street (Central Switchboard)
 (0624) 682000
Isle of Man Bank, Atholl Street (0624) 842122
Lloyds, Douglas Street (0624) 842203
Tourist Information
Peel Bus Depot (0624) 842349

ST JOHN'S

Inland and to the East of Peel is St John's. Dotted about the Guide are various references to the politically important role that this pretty village has played and continues to play to this very day in the life of the Isle of Man. Sitting comfortably with an air of elegance, hugging the gap between *Slieau Whallian* and *Beary Mountain* – traced back to the Scandinavian for Farm of the Shieling – it is well worth a visit. Every 5th July, all roads lead to St John's. On this our National Day the Island celebrates over a thousand years of unbroken government by holding the traditional open air Tynwald. Thousand upon thousands of Islanders and visitors make the journey to watch the ancient ceremony. The laws of Mann which have been enacted during the last year are proclaimed in Manx and English, in summarised form, by the Deemsters – Manx equivalent to the British High Court Judges – to the gathered public, after which Tynwald has a formal meeting within the Royal Chapel of St John's. Sitting at a lofty height above the throngs and on the summit of Tynwald Hill is the Lieutenant Governor. Below him and arranged in descending order are variously the Keys, Legislative Council, Crown Officers, Churchmen, Heads of Local Authorities, Captains of the Parishes and the six Coroners of the Island. The formal part of the day is supported by a Fair and a good time is had by all!

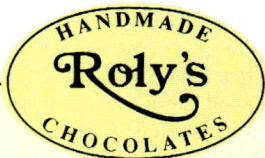

Delicious luxury hand-made chocolates using Belgian chocolate. Choose from Pralines featuring smooth hazelnut paste, Truffles made from fresh cream ganache enhanced with real liqueurs or butter cream centres such as pistachio, passion fruit & banana. All available in white, milk or plain chocolate. Unique sculptured animal shapes and Manx Heritage scenes including Laxey Wheel make lovely gifts as do the delightfully crisp after-dinner mints featuring the 3-legs of Mann. (Heritage shapes available at all Manx Museum sites).

Roly's at the Tynwald Craft Centre
(23 craft shops at St. Johns)
☎ **801752**
Open 10–5pm Mon–Sat and 2–5pm Sundays

Tynwald Craft Centre
Tynwald Mills, St Johns
Tel: 801213
Open Normal Hours All Year Round

Your holiday shopping and gift ideas couldn't be easier – with over 20 retail outlets there's something for everyone. Spend the whole day browsing whilst the children enjoy our adventure playground and when you find that you have worked up an appetite – or you're just dying for a coffee, the cafe fits the bill perfectly.

This extensive complex centred around a vast mill shop provides manufacturing – shopping – heritage gifts – exhibitions – and features a perfumery & skincare factory – aquaria & ponds – model trains – toy shop – gift shops – book shop – conservation centre – lingerie – dried flowers – furnishings – lighting – fabrics – cafe/restaurant – artists gallery – handmade chocolates – heritage products – woodcrafts – a pottery – garden centre and more. The Tynwald Centre provides free on site parking and is also serviced regularly by bus and coach.

– A COMPLETE EXPERIENCE FOR ALL –

One of the most popular developments of recent years has seen the site of the old Tynwald Woollen Mills change from just the production of fine woollen garments into a full blown craft and shopping centre. Now known as the Tynwald Craft Centre the visitor can choose from a range of over twenty shops, offering everything from model trains, confectionery, fancy goods, clothing, furniture, dried flowers, home decor, light fittings, art-work, ceramics, books, souvenirs, woodcraft, to perfumes, skin care and lots more. Many of the shops export their goods worldwide and the expertise of the various representative companies is much sought after at home and abroad. A special mention must be made here of Roly's Chocolates. This small shop turns out hand made exquisite chocolates using the finest materials from Belgium. Roly's are able to design chocolates to a customer's own requirements, and a visit to Tynwald Mills would not be complete without calling into this lovely shop.

There is plenty of parking at the complex and it is on the bus routes and coach tour itineraries. Children are catered for with play areas and there are excellent catering facilities. A visit is highly recommended.

KIRK MICHAEL

Now using the shortened version of its name, it was previously known as Kirk Michael Towne or Michaeltown. Fame comes to this sunny village at least twice a year as the racing motorcycles flash through the main road at incredible mind boggling speeds. TT mythology tells that the inhabitants of Kirk Michael have the flattest feet in the Isle of Man by reason of the houses edging right up to the race course... the writer doesn't think it is true, but the inhabitants do put up with the road closures in a very gracious manner. There are some interesting shops spaced out along the main road and if you are interested in antiques, save some time to visit Philip Morrison's shop. The warm and friendly greeting you receive ensures that you feel comfortable looking in the nooks and crannies for that much sort after piece of furniture or ornament.

Glen Wyllin, sometimes spelt without a break between the words, means Mill Glen, was once a famous tourist attraction much helped by the railway. Nothing remains of the railway now except two lonely sandstone support pillars for the old bridge which they used to carry high above the Glen. None

PHILIP MORRISON
Antiques

Church View House
Kirk Michael
Isle of Man
Tel: (0624) 878433

— . —

ALSO AT

BACCHUS WINES
7 CLINCH'S NORTH QUAY
DOUGLAS
ISLE OF MAN
TEL: (0624) 663319

Member of The London & Provincial
Antiques Dealers Association

BALLACARNANE FARM

FOR A HOLIDAY WITH A DIFFERENCE, ONE YOU'LL NEVER FORGET, WHY NOT LET US MAKE YOU WELCOME ON OUR FARM ON THE WEST COAST

Modern and well appointed property with outstanding views overlooking the Irish Sea to Ireland and Scotland. 5 Bedrooms (Sleeps 10), Lounge, Dining Room, Modern Kitchen with all WM/DW/Micro. etc. Gas Fired C/H. Garden. Send for further details now for that perfect holiday on the Island.

TELEPHONE: 0624 878261
Ballacarnane Farm, Michael, Isle of Man IM6 1HN

2 NIGHT HOLIDAYS FROM £66

EVERYMANN'S ISLE OF MAN

Everymann is the Isle of Man Department of Tourism's very own tour operator and offers the best combination of quality, value and choice to suit your pocket. We know the Island best and in 1993 welcomed our 170,000th visitor to our Island.

Everymann will make your Isle of Man holiday even more enjoyable. There's so much to choose from with Evérymann and you'll also benefit from special discounts, reduced admissions and concessions on your travel in the Isle of Man.

Every hotel and guest house we offer has been vetted to ensure it represents a high standard in its category, with a large selection of accommodation from small friendly guest houses to high quality hotels.

We know you are looking forward to a trouble-free holiday or special weekend break. Going with Everymann Holidays gives you full security and the knowledge that you are booking with the Isle of Man holiday specialists. Why settle for less when you can go with Everymann and know you're getting value for money.

You will find all the details including some very special offers in the Everymann Holiday Brochure. It's available from your local ABTA travel agent.

Booking with Everymann is simplicity itself. Sit back and enjoy a leisurely look through the Everymann Brochure. You'll find plenty to tempt you to visit the Isle of Man. Your local travel agent will be happy to make all the arrangements, check availability and help you to complete your booking form, or call the Everymann Central Reservations Office yourself on **0624 629914**

Everymann HOLIDAYS

Send us the coupon or telephone 0624 629914 or fax 0624 627514.

To Everymann Holidays, Centaurman House, 20a Duke Street, Douglas, Isle of Man.

My special interest is:
- ☐ Family Holidays   ☐ Walking   ☐ Heritage   ☐ Tours
- ☐ Railway   ☐ Fishing   ☐ Over 55's Holidays
- ☐ Special Activities ☐ Golf   ☐ Water Sports
- ☐ Romantic Weekend Breaks   ☐ Tailor-made Holidays

NAME _____

ADDRESS _____

_____

_____ Postcode _____

of the beauty has been lost however and happy days can still be had down on the beach, and there are plenty of pleasant walks in the neighbourhood.

Churchyards, as with all burial grounds, are the providers of a potted history of bygone days and Kirk Michael's is no exception. Within these hallowed grounds are buried five bishops. There is a memorial stone to that much loved priest, "The Good" Bishop Wilson. This kind and generous hearted man did much for the people of Ellan Vannin in his long and beneficial stewardship of the Christian faith. It is reputed that prior to his death an elm tree was cut down to provide the wood for his coffin. Bishop Wilson planted that tree when he first arrived on the Island to take up this great office some fifty seven years earlier.

BALLAUGH

The Parish from which the village takes its name measures some five miles in a North to South Line and about three miles from East to West. The boundaries touch Jurby to the North, Michael and Lezayre to the South and East. It is the beginning of the scenery that is so typical of this corner of the Island where the lonely glens run down to the low sandy cliffs of the shore against a background of the northern mountains and hills. The modern village is some way from the sea, straddling the main Peel to Ramsey road and you clearly see the new church – built 1832 – from afar. Approximately a mile and a half nearer the sea lies old Kirk Ballaugh Church with its very distinctive "leaning" gate posts. Parish Registers are still an important source of information

---

SARTFIELD FARMHOUSE
LICENSED RESTAURANT AND CAFE

Good farmhouse fare in friendly surroundings at prices you can afford
• Meals • Snacks • Afternoon Tea • A la Carte
Open every day – signposted from the Barre Garrow crossroads on the TT Course near Kirk Michael

TELEPHONE: 878280

Old Ballaugh Church

Jurby Church

imagined by reading the inscriptions on the old headstones and the church porch has a fine collection of stone crosses. In the new part of the churchyard, the well kept graves of the Polish, Canadian, Anzac and British airmen who made the ultimate sacrifice, are laid out in neat rows. On a clear day, stand at the back of the church. The Mull and its lighthouse seem almost as if they could be touched and if you listen carefully... you can hear the silence!

Andreas has always been a pleasant village much enjoying its peaceful rural existence, largely uninterrupted since the end of the Viking era. In the 1940s, the land to the North and West of the village was utilised as an RAF base and the villagers became used to great flying machines overhead at all times of day and night. Roads and lanes which had previously only been wide enough to suit a horse and cart were enlarged, and it was not an unusual sight to see large aircraft being manoeuvred about on the roads skirting the edge of this ancient village. The heady days of the wartime emergency over, Andreas quickly reverted to its placid ways.

For the lover of architecture the Parish Church of Kirk Andreas with its Lombardic campanile is unexpected, but the Italian style sits well and at ease in the Manx countryside. It was built in 1802 to replace a church from the thirteenth century, the time when parishes were first formed on the Island. There was great excitement in 1869 when Anglo-Saxon coins were discovered during the building of the bell tower. Dedicated to St Andrew, probably during the period of Scottish Rule circa 1275 to 1334, there are indications that suggest a much earlier church, whose name has been lost, occupied the site. During the Second World War the spire was removed from the church to give a clear flight path for the planes using RAF Jurby and RAF Andreas. The Andreas carved stones are very fine examples of the craftsmanship of those far off days and one, a pillar, is particularly interesting with its inscription in Roman capitals and letters from the Ogham alphabet. Such carvings were seldom found outside of Wales. The Grosvenor Hotel in the centre of the village is the northernmost public house in the Island and when you have finished your explorations and need refreshment, pay them a visit, you will not be disappointed.

Sitting on the slopes of the Bride Hills, the village

and Ballaugh has the oldest in the Island dating from 1598. If you visit this consecrated place, look at the bog oak notice board enumerating the rectors back to the earliest days of the fifteenth century.

JURBY, ANDREAS AND BRIDE

These, the three northern most Parishes fall within the Sheadings of Michael and Ayre respectively. They share virtually the same scenery and the only high ground in the area is found in the shape of the Bride Hills. Very much farming country, the northern plain is a maze of roads and lanes zigzagging between the villages. Although well signposted, it is easy to get lost but a quick look over your shoulder towards the mountains will soon put you back on course.

Jurby in more modern times grew up around the old Air Force base and, although now closed, good use is being made of the site with various small businesses based there. A visit to the old garrison church is worth a diversion and if you have time, wander through the churchyard. There is a lot of history to be

Manx Cottage

of Bride seems almost becalmed in a haven of peace. It has known troubled times though, and its earlier history can best be described as turbulent. Frequently the victims of raids by pirates and marauders, the poor inhabitants often went in fear of their very lives. There is a Manx ballad which gives the origins of the old tradition that the people of Kirk Bride always used to eat their meat course before the soup. On clear summer days the smoke from the Bride chimneys could be seen from the Galloway coast and the story is told that the villainous chieftain Cutlar MacCulloch and his men would, on seeing this, set sail for a good Manx feed. On one occasion arriving at a wedding feast just after soup had been taken, they devoured the meat prepared for the guests. The incident is celebrated in verse form.

The rovers were many, the wedding guests few,
So the rovers sat down to the mutton and stew,
But from that day to this, as our North custom tells,
We trust neither to wind, nor to mermaid spells,
But first of all eat – our coveted meat,
And over the broth tell of MacCulloch's feat.

Marked clearly on the map to the West of Bride is Thurot Cottage, a private house whose building was made possible by utilising timbers from the defeated French Men of War lead by the "Bellisle", under the command of Captain Thurot. This battle was witnessed by Bishop Hildesley in February 1760 and would in all likelihood have been seen and certainly heard from Bride. There is a car park besides the road below the church and there are a number of pleasant walks to be enjoyed in the neighbourhood.

Annual Manx Language Summer School

Every year, there is a Manx Language Summer School, held in the Isle of Man in the first two weeks of August.

If you would like to learn some Manx (or some more Manx) in a pleasant and relaxed atmosphere, this is for you. You can learn about other aspects of Manx culture as well, such as Manx music and songs. If you want, you can take part in social events associated with the Summer School.

You can find out more from: Brian Stowell, 16 Hilary Road, Douglas, Isle of Man IM2 3EG, British Isles. Phone: (Isle of Man) 623821.

RAMSEY

Distances Ballasalla 24, Castletown 26, Douglas 16, Laxey 8, Peel 16, Port Erin 28, Port St Mary 28.

The Chronicles of Mann in about 1250 have the northern town recorded as *Ramsa* seemingly drawn from the old Scandinavian language. In the Manorial Roll of 1703 the current and English spelling of the name is indicated. The Manx Gaelic has it as *Ramsaa* which on closer inspection is similar to Ramsa, the Scandinavian for Wild Garlic River. Old OS maps however show the river as *Stroon ny Craue,* Manx for The Stream of the Wild Garlic.

There are no buildings of great antiquity in Ramsey save for old Ballure Church. The Burial Register dates from 1611 and the building was reported in 1637 to be in a near ruinous state, but over the years at various times it has been restored. Bishop Wilson held a thanksgiving service here to celebrate deliverance from the French and to honour Commodore Elliot's victory. Ramsey in the last decade or so has been trying to decide whether to go for a totally modern style of rebuild or aim for a blend of the old with the new. In fact it is probably towards the latter they are drifting and there is a happy mingling of architectural styles, particularly on the sea front.

Presumably the reason for much of Ramsey's lack of old buildings lies in the fact that it was the site of much destruction across the centuries. Olaf, King of Mann, was murdered by his nephew Reginald near the harbour in 1154. Somerled, the twelfth century Thane of Argyll, made a historic landing here, and Robert the Bruce a century later passed through on his way to besiege Castle Rushen. The prestigious prefix to the name must have been hard earned and it most likely evolved from the fact that Ramsey was the gateway of kings long before the coming of Godred Crovan in 1079. Landing in Ramsey became a lot easier when the magnificent Ramsey Pier was built. Thrusting itself out into deep water it quickly became a popular stopping off point for the steamers en route to other ports of call. At the present it is closed for repairs and the future hopefully will be one that ensures its well being.

Situated at the mouth of the Sulby River, Ramsey

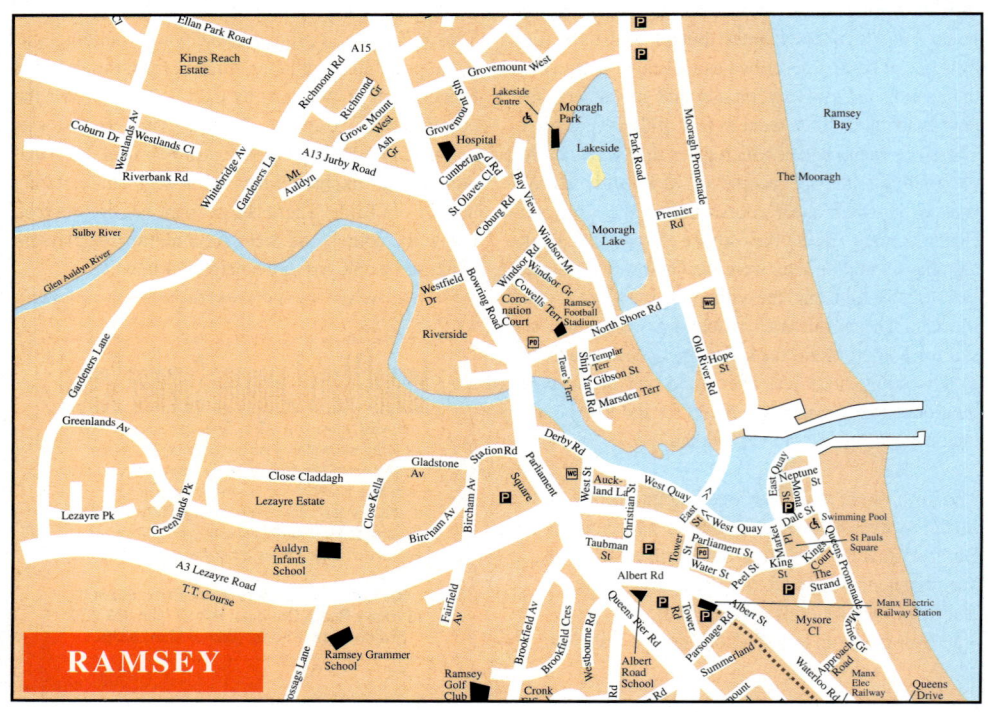

Ramsey

was undoubtedly an island. In 1630 the town was virtually destroyed by the sea, a continuous threat that the townsfolk were to live with and suffer from, until the early years of the nineteenth century. From the re-direction of the river and the silting up of the old harbour entrance, good was to come. As a result, Ramsey now possesses the enchanting Mooragh Park. The harbour is pure joy for anyone even remotely interested in water activities. Across the harbour the Ramsey shipyard has built many fine vessels, the most famous of which the "Star of India" is a famous attraction in the American port city of San Diego. Ramsey's shipyard can also claim to have played a major part in the development of the oil business by building the world's first two ships specifically designed as oil tankers.

Many people are now finding their way to the sunniest part of the Island and using it as a holiday base. The pace of life on the Isle of Man is generally much slower than that of the adjacent isles and it is fair to say that Ramsey's way of life is even more relaxed than the rest of Ellan Vannin. There is much to do and see in this market town. Shopping is effortless and if you are like everyone else on holiday, you tend to window shop before taking the plunge and purchasing holiday presents. Edwina Ely is a shop that needs a visit, they have so much inside that to miss it of the shopping list would be nothing short of foolish. They have a variety of china, linen and lots of wonderful ideas for gifts... and don't worry if you can't carry it home they do have a mail order department. Eating out is not difficult in the capital of the North, most of the pubs and hotels offer bar meals. Moving out of Ramsey is easy by public transport but to make it easier still, Raymotors in Parliament Square have a good selection of Ford cars for hire. Hopefully there will be no problems with your own car whilst on holiday but it is a comforting thought that the skilled team at Raymotors could look after you, should the need arise.

If you really want a relaxing holiday, the 4-star Grand Island Hotel situated high above the water's edge at the far end of the Mooragh Promenade will provide all the ingredients. Here you can spoil yourself and indulge in all the activities that you have been promising yourself that you would do... when you had time! If it makes you feel better or you need the exercise, there is always the Henley Club to get

RAC ★★★★　　　　　　　　　　**♛♛♛♛♛ COMMENDED**

THE GRAND ISLAND HOTEL
RAMSEY, ISLE OF MAN
Tel: 0624-812455   Fax: 0624-815291

The Island's only 4-star Hotel
55 en-suite rooms. Health Club.
Indoor Swimming Pool. Jacuzzi, Snooker-room.
Resident Beautician and Hairdresser. Superb food. Magnificent views

Port of Ayre Lighthouse

you back in trim. Stress in your life is causing you problems? There is a bonus to staying at the Grand Island, the Managing Director Trevor Davies is a Clinical Hypnotherapist and Stress Counsellor and a period in his care will soon put the spring back into your life. This privately owned hotel, with individually designed bedrooms, extensive leisure facilities, beauty centre and its caring and friendly staff ensure that guests return again and again.

Before leaving Ramsey and its environs, it is worth pointing out that if your leaning is towards an action type of holiday, the Venture Centre at Lewaigue Farm, Maughold, could provide the outlet for any surplus energy. The Venture Centre is the Island's premier outdoor centre providing a wide range of adventure activities for the more agile visitor. Activities include archery, abseiling, air rifle shooting, assault course, canoeing, climbing, clay pigeon shooting, grass skiing and sailing. They offer full residential courses for both children and adults; half and full day activities are available for visitors staying elsewhere on the Island. Activities for one to one hundred persons can be provided and at substantial group discounts. Getting to the Venture Centre is easy by car or you can use the Manx Electric Railway, they have a halt close by.

Public Amenities

Harbour Master's Office (0624) 812245
Police Station (0624) 812234
Ramsey Cottage Hospital (0624) 813254
Ramsey Town Commissioners (Town Hall) (0624) 812228
Ramsey Post Office, Gladstone Park (0624) 812248
Ramsey Post Office, North Ramsey (0624) 813140

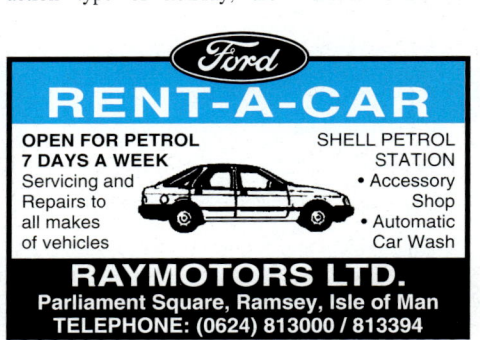

Ramsey

Towns and Villages

THE VENTURE CENTRE

MAUGHOLD, ISLE OF MAN, IM7 1AW

The Isle of Man's Premier Outdoor Activity Centre

- Children's Summer Camps
- Family & Group Activities
- Children's Adventure Days

Fun for all – young and old

Canoeing Abseiling, Climbing Sailing, Assault Course, Grass Skiing, Archery, Air rifle & Clay Pigeon Shooting etc.

For colour brochure & full programme details tel (0624) 814240

Banks
Barclays, Parliament Street (0624) 813124
Isle of Man Bank, Parliament Street (0624) 812829
Lloyds, Parliament Street (0624) 812225
Midland, St Paul's Square (0624) 814000
TSB Bank, Parliament Street (0624) 813596
Building Societies
Britannia (IOM), Market Square (0624) 816733
Leisure Centres
The Ventre Centre (Maughold) (0624) 814240
Mooragh Park (0624) 813375
Ramsey Swimming Pool, Queens Promenade (0624) 812852
Tourist Information
Ramsey Bus Depot (0624) 812151
Ramsey Electric Railway Station (Seasonal) (0624) 812249

Mooragn Park

Laxey

LAXEY

Distances Ballasalla 17, Castletown 20, Douglas 8, Peel 19, Port Erin 23, Port St Mary 24, Ramsey 8.

Salmon River or *Laxey* as we know it, has represented the Island on so many magazine covers, brochures, photographs, newspaper articles, radio and television programmes that it has become as synonymous with the Isle of Man as our famous kippers or the TT Races. Built up over the centuries the village sprawls along the sides of a deep glen, running down from the mine workings in its upper reaches, to the tiny harbour at the North end of a wide bay. Our Viking friends found Laxey to be a bountiful stopping of place on their roamings, hence the name.

Old papers of village life record that in the eighteenth century large shipments of fish were sent from the port to Sicily. In present times the main products are flour, still manufactured on the site of the 1513 mill, woollen goods and the famous Meerschaum and Briar pipes. Laxey Pipes on the Quay, warmly welcome visitors to their factory and if you decide to treat yourself to a new pipe there are fifteen styles, and six finishes to the Meerschaum to choose from. If you are a D.I.Y. enthusiast why not treat yourself to a pipe carving kit. The biggest industry Laxey has ever had was the mines. Lead, copper, zinc and silver were wrenched from the cold, wet and dank ground. Highly profitable in their heyday, between the years 1876 to 1882 the Great Laxey Mines paid out the highest total in dividends of all their competitor lead mines in the British Isles. Earnings of this magnitude ensured a reasonable standard of living for the inhabitants. Now the village is a very pleasant place to live and it has seen considerable expansion in recent times.

See our world-renowned Meerschaum and Briar Pipes which were hand-made by our local craftsmen

Visit Laxey Pipes

See our full range of pipes and smokers' requisites in our new showroom.

Open 9am to 5pm Monday to Friday

THE QUAY, OLD LAXEY. TELEPHONE: 861074

One piece of past glory that remains unchanged is the "Lady Isabella". Standing aloof from the purpose for which it was designed the biggest working water wheel in the world still performs its functions, much as it did from the first day of operation back in 1854. Named after the Governor of the day's wife, it is a stark reminder of the hard work that went into winning Laxey's wealth, pumping water from as much as two thousand feet below ground. The dimensions of the wheel are formidable with a circumference of 227 feet and ninety five steps lifting you up to the platform 75 feet from the ground. Can you imagine ending your shift at the bottom of the mine and climbing up ladders, one hundred feet in length to the surface. Little wonder the mine owners didn't object when the men requested permission to work "double shifts". Manx National Heritage have done an excellent job of interpreting life as it was in the mines and the mine trail is a must for every visitor. On a fine day take a picnic and enjoy the sense of the past.

Lower down the Glen there are plenty of activities for young and old. There are gardens and the beach for the children to enjoy, whilst the older tourist can take in the small folk museum near the station or use the time to take a trip up Snaefell. Hunger is a subject you need never experience in Laxey. There are a number of eating houses and pubs that will keep you going, just keep an eye open for the Okell's Falcon, the sign of good food, wines and ales.

Public Amenities
Harbour Master's Office (0624) 861663
Laxey Commissioners (Town Hall) (0624) 861241
Laxey Post Office (0624) 861209
Police Station (not continuously manned)
 (0624) 861210, (0624) 631212
Banks
Isle of Man Bank, New Road (0624) 861201
Tourist Information
Electric Railway Station (Seasonal) (0624) 861226
Electric Railway Sub-Station (0624) 861244
Laxey Heritage Information Centre, Mines Road
 (0624) 862007

Snaefell Mountain Railway

ONCHAN

The patron saint of the Parish of Onchan was St Christopher, better known by his Gaelic name of *Conchenn,* meaning Dog-Head or Wolf-Head. There is a strong case to be argued that the name of the village is identified with St Connachan, who was Bishop of Sodor and Man in 540 AD. Remarkably within the porch of St Peter's Church there are three cross slabs which depict dog-like monsters. The present church built in 1833 has no particular style of architecture but within the churchyard there are many interesting graves amongst them being that of Lieutenant Edward Reeves RN, one of Nelson's officers who fought with him at Trafalgar. The earlier church on this site witnessed the marriage of Captain Bligh of "Bounty" fame to a Manx girl, Elizabeth Betham, daughter of the Collector of Customs on the Island. Bligh was reputed to have rued the day that he came to the Isle of Man and met up with Fletcher Christian. Although the Church Register is not the oldest on the Island, it does date back to 1627 and perusal of the list of vicars commences with one appointed in 1408.

In Church Road at the place known as "The Butt" there is a quaint building with a carved head over the door. Known as Molly Caroon's cottage it was formerly used as a mission hall. Now restored it is occasionally opened to the public so that they may sample a taste of Manx tradition. The old part of the village is grouped around the church, but with Onchan expanding so rapidly in recent years, with a number of large estates spread around the hilly countryside, the village has the second largest centre of population on the Island. A new landmark is the King Edward Bay clubhouse serving a challenging and very demanding golf course laid out on the hilly terrain of Banks Howe.

Towns and Villages

Douglas Bay

At the North end of Douglas Bay above the cliffs at Port Jack stands Onchan's only residential hotel. Run by Glynn Noon, The Park Hotel undoubtedly has the finest panoramic views of Douglas Bay. This well appointed hotel with a cocktail bar and restaurant offer table d'hote or full à la carte menus. Increasingly popular with the business visitor, The Park Hotel is only minutes away from many amenities and the Island's business centre. Run by an ex seafarer, if ship memorabilia and tales of the sea are to your liking, a refreshing holiday staying here is for you. The hotel is an excellent base for exploring the Island and it has good car parking facilities. Don't worry if you have not brought your car as the hotel is close to bus routes, and the Manx Electric Rail and horse tram termini are just down the road. Only a few yards away is Onchan Park where you can enjoy boating, tennis, bowls, pitch 'n put golf, or the frequent stock car races.

THE PARK HOTEL

**1-3 ROYAL AVENUE
PORT JACK
ONCHAN**

TEL : (0624) 676906
FAX : (0624) 676398

APPROVED

The Park Hotel is ideally situated overlooking Douglas Bay. All public rooms and most bedrooms enjoy spectacular views. Relax and enjoy your holiday in this well appointed hotel, with full central heating, telephones, radio room call and Satellite TV.
Facilities include charming cocktail bar, Garden Lounge and the Regency Restaurant which offers table d'hote or full range a la carte menus.
Situated only minutes from the main amenities including Summerland, Onchan Park and the Electric Railway. Regular Horse Trams to central Douglas close to hotel..

Herring Tower, Langness

BEACHES, LEISURE AND ENTERTAINMENT GUIDE

SAFETY AT SEA
* **Know where your children are at all times.** Keep an eye on them, especially when they are swimming or playing on the water's edge. Children can drown even in very shallow water.
* **Make sure you always know where everyone else is.** Let each other know if anyone is going swimming or leaving the beach for any reason.
* **Beware of being trapped by the tide coming in.** You can find out about local currents by asking the local Harbour Master or the Coastguard, especially if you are going to a remote beach.
* **Don't play on rocks.** Take care on groynes and breakwaters – they can be dangerous.
* **Never climb on cliffs and keep away from cliff edges.** Even gentle slopes can be dangerous when they are wet.
* **Watch out for large waves coming in.** They can sweep you off your feet even if you think you are standing somewhere safe.
* **Always obey any notices or instructions.**

IN THE WATER
* Don't swim:
  – if you feel unwell.
  – for at least an hour after a meal (you may get cramp).
  – when you are cold or tired.
  – if you have been drinking alcohol.
* Always swim where there are other people.
* Always swim close to the beach and don't swim out to sea.
* Don't stay in the water too long. You will get cold and tired.
* Don't use inflatable airbeds in the water. They can get blown out to sea.
* If you have a belly board, stay with the board and don't go out too far.
* Only use a snorkel if you are a good swimmer and the water is calm. Don't snorkel if you have breathing problems.

TIDE INFORMATION
Tide times in the Isle of Man are based on high water Liverpool plus or minus the following difference:

Calf Sound + 0 05 mins   Douglas – 0 04 mins
Peel – 0 02 mins   Ramsey + 0 04 mins

Remember to add the hour for Summer Time. Tidal information can be obtained from the local press or from Manx Radio immediately following the weather forecasts.

WEATHER INFORMATION
Weather forecasts are broadcast regularly, particularly at news times, on Manx Radio courtesy of the Isle of Man Meteorological Office.
The frequencies used for Manx Radio are:
  1368 KHz AM . 89-97.2-103.7 MHz Stereo FM
Shipping Forecasts are broadcast daily by BBC Radio 4 (long wave 198 KHz 1515 M) at 05.55, 13.55, 17.50 and 00.33.
Weather Forecasts are broadcast by BBC Radio 4 at 06.03, 06.55, 07.55, 08.58, 12.55, 17.55, 21.59 and 00.20.
For further information on weather and tides in the Isle of Man, please contact the local Harbour Master in your area or Douglas Harbour Control.

BEACH GUIDE
For such a small Island there is a wide variety of choice when it comes to a day out on the beach. If you are an expert on sandcastles the range runs from the good bonding sand of Port Erin and Douglas beaches to the fine sand of Peel and the difficult to work with, dune sands of the North West beaches. Most beaches are safe but that always depends on the responsible attitude adopted by beach users… so please, always take care. There are many currents flowing around the Island's coastline and the dangerous waters of the Calf Sound and at the Point of Ayre are witness to that fact, and at least they are visible.

All beaches on the Isle of Man are owned by the Government up to the high water mark and there are no charges for their use. Some beaches are inaccessible,

Laxey

others are difficult to reach and with a mean tidal range of 24 feet it really does pay to keep an eye on the incoming tide. Where access to beaches is by means of the coastal footpath or across headlands, please remember the Isle of Man is very much a rural area and observe the code of the countryside.

On the East coast the sandy beaches commence at *Cranstal,* Treen or Homestead possibly belonging to someone called Kraun. Just a little further on is *Shellag Point,* Seal Creek or Bay, but any indentation of the shore disappeared long ago as a consequence of the continuous erosion of the coastline. Good fishing along this beach all the way into Ramsey. Ramsey has plenty of relaxation to offer and while Mum and Dad enjoy a break the youngsters can enjoy a sail or a canoe trip on the Mooragh Lake. The public park here close to Ramsey seafront, presents a number of amusements and remains a favourite place for tourists.

Excellent sandy beach from the South of the harbour entrance to *Port Lewaigue,* which means Creek. The other side of a headland known as *Gobny Rona,* Point of the Seal, has a nice beach in the pretty little cove of *Port e Vullen,* a name the meaning of which is lost in the mists of time. This is the last sandy beach until Laxey. Between Maughold Head and Laxey there are a number rocky coves with stoney beaches and whilst swimming is not recommended, they are a treat to visit with something on offer for all age groups.

Laxey beach and harbour will keep you well occupied. There is always something going on and even doing nothing can be a pleasant experience. Many people hop on the tram to Laxey and entertain themselves quite easily. A walk up the Glen Road makes a change from beach life and the Village Commissioners bowling green and tennis courts offer the opportunity of a little competitive exercise.

Across the bay from Laxey is Garwick Bay. There is a very rocky shore here and without doubt it is best to leave your vehicle on the main road above the beach and walk. The access road is very steep and should only be attempted if you are fit. Next stop is Groudle Beach which is reached by taking the minor slip road which is just up the hill from the main glen entrance. Groudle is making great efforts to recapture some of its old glories and leading the way is the Groudle Railway Company. If your hobby is trains, the miniature railway winding its way round the North headland gives immense pleasure.

Onchan suffers from a lack of beaches although it can lay claim to a couple of small inlets, one of which rejoices in the magnificent name of Onchan Harbour. Douglas can boast one of the finest sweeps of any bay in the British Isles. There are plenty of leisure activities in Douglas and if you need information on a wide range of sports and entertainment then the friendly staff at the Tourist Information Office, Discovery Guides or the hotel reception will be only to pleased to guide and advise you. Starting to the South of Port Jack the rocky beach soon gives way to almost one and a half miles of sand, fringed with a border of shingle. It offers endless hours of pleasure to all generations.

Leaving the sands of Douglas behind, the coastline offers many coves and inlets all the way down to Derbyhaven. Many are accessible by vehicle, some only on foot... all offer something different. Derbyhaven is now very much a water leisure centre, although there is an area of sandy beach towards the hotel on the North side of the Langness peninsula. If you are a golfer then play the famous Castletown Golf Links course. The 17th hole on this course is every bit as exciting as the famous Turnberry lighthouse hole.

Castletown beach although much smaller than Douglas has an imposing back drop, with the harbour, castle and town combining to give it a feeling of timelessness. The peace and quiet does get shattered on occasions such as in August when the World Tin Bath Championships are held in the harbour. During International Cycle Week a Kermess is held in the town which is a very exciting spectacle. To the South and West of the town the shoreline gives way to lava beds and rough, jagged, needle like rocks and it is not until you reach the bottom of Fishers Hill, A7, that a

Port Erin Beach

small sandy beach is again encountered. The western end of *Bay ny Carrickey* offers plenty of space to indulge in all sorts of water-borne or shore based activities and short walk round Gansey Point bring you to Chapel Bay, a children's playground for centuries.

The high cliffs between Port St Mary, The Sound and Port Erin prevent any kind of casual beach activity and they are best viewed from a boat or strictly left to the skilled rock climbers. During the summer months the local yachts provide entertainment as they dash about the bay. There are a number of well signposted footpaths covering the area but please remember cliff walking can be dangerous, especially in windy conditions.

Port Erin beach is best described as a jewel in the crown. Golden sands, rocky inlets, a small cave or two, boats and even its own beach lighthouse; it has everything to offer the beach lover. Make the most of the sand here, as apart from one or two strands of beach, the rest of the accessible foreshores from here to Peel are rock, shingle and boulder strewn.

The fine sand at Peel is very difficult to use for sand castles when dry, so the experts advise. This should not put you off Peel, far from it, just move a little closer to the water's edge, it is much more pliable. The beach at Peel is ideal for motorcycle sand races and it really comes to life when the Go-kart Grand Prix is run around the narrow streets.

From a little North of Peel it is possible with care and the right tidal conditions to embark on a beach walk, which if you have the energy, will bring you right along the water's edge to Ramsey. The first few miles are along gently sloping beaches bordered by badly eroding sandy cliff faces, then from Glen Mooar onwards, sand dunes. High up above the A3, past the Devil's Elbow in the direction of Kirk Michael is *Ballacarnane Farm,* Homestead of the Cairn. The land here, if it could speak would tell tales of great incidents in the history of this small land, stories that would make the very hairs stand up on the back of your neck. The land cannot speak for itself so nowadays the story telling is best left to those who know the area. The Cannell family of Ballacarnane have farmed there for centuries – Mr Cannell is Captain of the Parish – and now give visitors a special insight into the life of the area by offering space and freedom in pleasant rural surroundings from the comfort of the farm bungalow. Sleeping up to ten people it is an ideal situation for multi-generation family holidays or a for a peaceful escape from the pressures of modern life… and by the way, the stories are good too!

The nearer you get to the Point of Ayre the more the rambler notices an almost subtle change from dune country to tightly knitted heather clad fields and then onto steeply shelving stone beaches, as you round the Point. From *Cranstal* you are back to eroding sandy cliffs and the "last legs" of a very exhausting walk.

BEAUFORT WIND SCALE

FORCE	M.P.H.	WIND	SEA
0	0-1	Calm	Like a mirror
1	1-3	Light airs	Ripples
2	4-7	Light breeze	Wavelets
3	8-11	Gentle breeze	Large wavelets, crests begin
4	12-18	Moderate breeze	Small waves, white horses
5	19-24	Fresh breeze	Moderate waves
6	25-31	Strong breeze	Light waves form white foam crests
7	32-38	Near gale	Heaps up, foam blown in streaks
8	39-47	Gale	Long waves, more foam
9	48-54	Severe gale	High waves, crests roll over, spray affects visibility
10	55-63	Storm	Very high waves, heavy tumbling over-hanging crests foam covers surface. Visibility reduced
11	64-72	Violent storm	Exceptionally high waves. All crests blown; foam covers surface. Visibility reduced.
12	73-81	Hurricane	Air filled with foam and spray. Mountainous seas completely white. Visibility very reduced.

LEISURE AND ENTERTAINMENT

With over 200 different events and attractions taking place on the Island during the year there is a wide choice... something for everyone in fact. If you have a particular hobby or interest be sure to mention it when you request information prior to your visit.

Each year the Isle of Man tries to introduce new attractions into its already packed calender. There are of course many famous events that are firm favourites and whilst many of them need no introduction, the examples shown below may very well be helpful in planning a visit. The list of events shown is not comprehensive and is merely intended to be a guide to "What's on" in the Island.

Scanning through the list will hopefully wet your appetite and encourage you to consider a trip across the Irish Sea and join in the festivities. A Guide book such as this can do no more than act as a taster for the potential visitor. More detailed information can easily be obtained from the Isle of Man Department of Tourism, Leisure and Transport or associated offices.

TT Course looking towards Ramsey

JANUARY
Fell races and other local sporting events. Theatre entertainment in Douglas and Port Erin.

FEBRUARY
Local sport. Musical recitals.

MARCH
Art Festivals and Exhibitions. Open Darts Festival. Short circuit motorcycle racing and local sporting events.

APRIL
Art Exhibitions. Easter Football, Rugby and Athletic Festivals. Castle to Castle Coast Walk. Student Festival of Sport. Peel Sports Festival. Fell racing. Motorcycle racing at Jurby. Manx Music Festival.

MAY
Manx Pairs Golf. Fell racing. RACMSA National Hill Climb Championship.
RACMSA National Sprint Championship. International Whitsun Hockey Festival.
Theatre entertainment. Brass Brand Festival. TT Motorcycle Practices.

MANSAIL
0624 813375/814240
BOATS FOR HIRE:- *Canoes, rowing boats, pedaloes, sailing dinghies.*
TUITION AVAILABLE FOR: - *Canoeing, sailing, windsurfing*
All Based on shallow 12 acre lake
GROUP DISCOUNTS AVAILABLE

THE BOATHOUSE
MOORAGH PARK LAKE,
RAMSEY, IM8 3AP

JUNE

TT Motorcycle Races and full supporting programme. Isle of Man Steam Packet National Road Races. Manx International Cycle Week. Crown Green Bowling Festival. Mananan International Festival of Music and the Arts. *Laa Columb Killey,* St Columba's Day Fair in Arbory. Peel Kart Grand Prix.

JULY

Isle of Man Maritime Festival. Andreas Racing Association Motorcycle Road Races. Manx Airlines Great Three legged Race. Tynwald Day. The Great Santan Fayre. Southern 100 Road Races. St Marks Village Fair. *Yn Chruinnaght* (Inter Celtic Festival). Summer Spectacular from Isle of Man Railways. Port St Mary Lifeboat Day. International Football Festival. Southern Agriculture Show.

AUGUST

Mannin Art Group Annual Open Exhibition and Competition. Royal Manx Agricultural Society Summer Show. Carnival Dance Championships. Douglas Carnival. World Tin Bath Championships, Castletown. Manx Grand Prix Motorcycle Practices. Manx National Two Day Trial. International Viola Competition. Fell racing.

SEPTEMBER

Manx Grand Prix Motorcycle Races. Manx Two Day Event (Horse Trials). Crown Green Bowling Festival. Manx International Car Rally. International Open Chess Tournament. Manx Classic Car Races.

OCTOBER

Motorcycle Road Races, Jurby. Two Peaks Fun Run, Mountain Bikes and Fell Runners. Isle of Man Philatelic Federation Convention.

NOVEMBER

Villa Marina Concerts.

DECEMBER

Isle of Man Railways, Santa Trains. Groudle Railway Mince Pie Trains. Christmas usually sees a pantomime or show in the Gaiety Theatre.

DAYS OUT BY CAR

MYLCHREESTS DRIVE 1

Douglas: Signpost Corner: The Bungalow: Ramsey: Maughold: Port Mooar: Port Cornaa: Dhoon: Laxey

Miles 35

As the vast majority of the Island's visitors stay on or near Douglas seafront, we will start Drive 1 at the foot of Broadway, which is adjacent to the Villa Marina or just about where the Harris Promenade merges with Central Promenade.

The Villa Marina has been in the forefront of the Manx tourism scene for many decades, putting on from time to time shows, stars of music and dancing, ballroom dancing and popular family entertainment. Built on land donated by a much loved citizen of the town, one Henry Bloom Noble who as a young man acting on his own initiative bought a cargo of timber for his employer, who was away on business. Alas for the employer he repudiated the young Noble's deal and thus set him on his way as a rival to fame and fortune with the proceeds of the sale of what had now become his goods. It's a good place to start our drive. The gardens at the Villa are attractive. A popular place for the visitor to watch the world pass by is from the roof of the Villa Marina Colonnade, entrance being gained from the gardens.

Climbing up Broadway we start to leave the tourist part of town behind and as Broadway becomes Ballaquayle Road we find ourselves at the Bray Hill traffic lights – turn right and head past the TT Grandstand (on your right). Some three quarters of a mile along Glencrutchery Road you arrive at Governor's Bridge. Be careful here that you don't turn too quickly, follow the road marked Ramsey turning up by the white painted stone wall. For the next few hundred yards on the right you are passing the home of the Island's Governor. Head on up the A18 to Signpost Corner, it's open country after this. Leaving Cronk-ny-Mona behind there is a distinct change of scenery starting to take place as the road winds upwards to the famous TT viewing spot of

TOUR 1

Creg-ny-Baa. Over to your left as Kate's Cottage comes into sight are some very good views of Douglas and the panorama of the southern half of the Isle of Man lies before you. Please be very careful where you stop to view, especially on the TT Course as it is a very fast road. Passing through Keppel Gate you are now in the mountains and into some of the finest scenery in the British Isles.

Still on the A18 we start our descent to Ramsey at Brandywell, just past the junction with the B10. Directly in front of you stands proud Snaefell and if time permits it is well worth stopping here and catching an electric tram to the summit. It is a fact that on a clear day seven Kingdoms can be seen from the top of the mountain. Not sure if this isn't a Manx fairy tale? Well, there before you lie the Kingdoms of England, Wales, Scotland, Ireland, Mann, the Kingdom of the Sea... and the Kingdom of Heaven. Past Snaefell the magnificent mountain scenery continues with the views on your right of Laxey and its valley gradually giving way to the stunning sight of Ramsey and the northern plain spreading out before you. Ramsey is a place well worth exploring

Ramsey Harbour

and as ever Mylchreests cars are supplied with parking discs just in case you don't find a disc free park. If you are driving your own vehicle, discs are available on the ferries, from TIC's or many public offices and police stations.

Maughold is the next stop on our itinerary and we find our way there by driving along Ramsey Promenade and past the Queen's Pier, watching for the signs directing traffic to Laxey A2. We are not on the A2 for long before we bear left onto the A15. A good tip on these roads is to watch out for the unmanned tram crossings as you will be criss-crossing them for the next few miles. About half a mile past Maughold there is a small road which takes you down onto the beach at Port Mooar. Don't expect to find any ships here but you will find peace and tranquillity. It's an ideal place to stretch your legs and have a picnic. Back up from the beach we turn left onto the A15 and travel to Cornaa.

If you like ancient monuments there is a well preserved burial ground just past the Ballajora crossroads – there is an old chapel on the corner –

Ramsey – Parliament Street

North Barrule

which in more recent times became the last resting place for those Quakers who remained on the Island, the majority of their fellow believers escaping persecution by seeking a new life in America. Careful navigation is required approaching Cornaa as the roads are very narrow. Turn off the A15 at Cornaa tram halt and turn down the minor road to the left. Pass the Ballaglass Glen car park on your right and drive on until you reach a small ford where you turn right for Port Cornaa. This is a very tight corner and you may feel happier by driving up the road a little way to turn. The drive down to the beach is well worth the effort but be careful where you park, it is a popular spot with locals and sometimes the stoney upper beach can cause problems if you pick the wrong place.

When coming back up this lovely wooded valley continue past the ford – on your right – and climb back up onto the A2 watching out for the signs to the Dhoon and Laxey. If you are feeling energetic park opposite the Dhoon station and enjoy a walk down to the shore but remember to leave extra time for the return journey… it can kid you. The A2 soon takes the happy traveller to Laxey and there are spectacular views all along the coast. Laxey has so much to offer that anything less than a prolonged visit borders on neglect. Enjoy the village because there is something new to see on each visit. There is a choice on how you leave. If you are in Old Laxey then the steep road up from the harbour soon comes out on the A2 at Fairy Cottage, or if you have been exploring in the vicinity of the mines then rejoin by the Electric Railway station. On through the picturesque villages of Lonan, Garwick and Baldrine and over the tram crossing just out of Baldrine, taking a left turn and over a second crossing in the vicinity of the Halfway House to Laxey (Liverpool Arms) – the road A11 is signposted to Groudle and Douglas. Groudle is another good place to while away a happy hour or two with its beautiful natural glen and the revitalised miniature Groudle Railway. Almost home but not finished with the scenery. Stop a while and drink in the sight of beautiful Douglas Bay. Day or night, you will enjoy the view.

Maughold Crosses

MYLCHREESTS DRIVE 2

Douglas: East Baldwin: Injebreck: Druidale: Ballaugh: Kirk Michael: Peel: St. John's

Miles 38

This journey takes as its starting point the bottom of Broadway and proceeds in just the same manner as that described in Drive 1, until the traffic lights at Parkfield Corner are reached. Get into the filter left lane and enjoy the run down Bray Hill to the bottom of the dip where you take a right turn – it's easy to spot – look out for Bradley's grocery shop. Allow yourself a brief thought for the racing motor cyclists as they speed down that hill at over 150 mph!

The road now winds along through an area known as *Port-e-Chee*, which translated from the Gaelic means Haven of Peace, and it needs little imagination to realise that this place may well have been, in pre-glacial times, the site of one of the earliest harbours in the Isle of Man. Cronkbourne Village is the next destination and this is soon reached. Turn right and go up the steep Johnny Watterson's Lane A21 turning left at the halt sign, then drive along Ballanard Road A22 towards Abbeylands for just over a mile. At the crossroads turn left and heading over Sir George's Bridge make a right turn onto the B21, the East Baldwin Road.

It is very hard to imagine that between 1900-05 a narrow gauge railway wound its way around these small valleys busily carrying building materials for the Injebreck Reservoir.

Keep on the B21 and move in a northerly direction until you reach the old and disused East Baldwin Chapel. Park here awhile and if you are not blessed with sharp eyes use binoculars to see if you can spot "The White Man of East Baldwin". The "White Man" is a figure built into a mountain wall on the hillside as a memorial to a Deemster, who perished with his horse in a snowstorm, whilst on an errand of mercy. The walk up to the cairn from the bottom of the valley is strenuous, and mind you don't get your feet wet when crossing the Baldwin River. Any physical discomfort experienced on the way up is soon overcome and the views are more than adequate compensation for the effort.

Retrace your track back to Algare Hill – it's the small connecting road between the two valleys – and a right turn at the top brings you along to St Luke's Church which is on the site of an ancient Tynwald. Drop down to the valley floor and join the B22 by heading once more in a northerly direction. Lots of nice picnic spots around here but do be careful where you park, the roads are narrow. If you like to fish

TOUR 2

Greeba Mountain from Crosby

Kirk Michael Church

becomes the A4 and we head down towards the sunset city of Peel. This is a good road but if you are not in a hurry then enjoy a flask of tea or coffee at Glen Wyllin, Glen Mooar or the Devil's Elbow. By now the visitor to our fair shores will have gathered that much of the beauty of the Island requires a Mylchreests car or your own vehicle to get the best out of a visit.

Peel is a place to visit with time to spend on exploring. This is the only "city" on the Island – two cathedrals – a title of which the good citizens are justly proud. Peel is close to every Manx person's heart so give yourselves time to soak up the atmosphere. Lots of interesting shops, narrow streets, a harbour and a very fine castle. If you are out on an evening run, stay for the sunset, you won't be disappointed.

Leaving Peel behind we take the A1 to St. John's, a village of great political importance in the lives of our modern nation. An alternative route to the village is via the A20 and the connecting road through Tynwald Mills... it is well signposted from Peel. Alongside Tynwald Hill and the memories of past deeds that it evokes, lies the Royal Chapel of St. John. The village is little changed in the best part of a century, representing as it does all the things that the Manx most cherish... freedom, law and order, and tradition.

The last part of the drive takes us along the central valley. Hard to imagine that a mere 10,000 years ago this was the sea bed, dividing the two main parts of the Isle of Man from each other. Moving along the A1 towards Ballacraine we come up against that rarity in the Island, a set of traffic lights. Carry straight on towards Douglas but just after Greeba Castle look to your left and there is the ancient roofless church of St. Trinian standing in splendid isolation in its own meadow. There is a choice of routes to the capital from here on.

The main road follows the A1 to the Sea Terminal via Glen Vine, Union Mills, Braddan Bridge, and the Quarter Bridge. Alternatively if time permits why not take the A23, the Nab Road, by turning left at Crosby and heading towards Douglas via Eyreton, the Nab, the Strang and Braddan – the A23 rejoins the A1 at the Jubilee Oak Braddan Bridge. If it's dark when arriving back in the metropolis, enjoy the promenade lights.

then the appropriate licences are available from the Douglas TIC, Department of Agriculture, Fisheries and Forestry or some local Post Offices... and Injebreck is as good a place as anywhere to indulge. From the reservoir the road climbs up between the peaks of Colden and Carraghan eventually bringing you onto the Brandywell Road B10. Just before the junction there is a small slip road which you should turn into and, by turning right and then almost straight away left, you are now on the Druidale Road. This is a single track road for its entire length. If you decide to stop and admire the views, park the car to one side and please watch out for sheep and cattle... they have the run of the range up here on the moors. A short drive down Ballaugh Glen brings the traveller to the village.

Turning left at the famous Ballaugh Bridge puts you onto the A3. The car driver has the advantage over the TT riders because at least the wheels stay firmly on the ground – the leather clad heroes are airborne for quite a distance here. Now we are heading South West towards Kirk Michael, home of Runic Crosses and the last resting place of no less than five bishops. Take the right fork here as the A3

Looking towards Snaefell

MYLCHREESTS DRIVE 3

Ramsey: Point of Ayre: Jurby: The Cronk: The Curraghs: Sulby: Tholt-e-Will: The Bungalow

Miles 38

For those visitors staying in Ramsey there are many pleasant drives to enjoy in the close vicinity of this small market town. The drive described in the following few paragraphs will just emphasise the kaleidoscope of choice that faces the visitor to Ellan Vannin. A car makes that choice all the more exciting and the writer feels and hopes that in the few miles described in Drive 3 the tourist will feel something about the changeability of the Island that can only best be described as the "Magic of Mann".

As you wander around the great northern plain the scenery changes frequently, from the fine sands of the Lhen, gravel beaches of the Point of Ayre, up to the wooded slopes of Sky Hill, Glen Auldyn, *Carrick*, Rock and *Mount Karrin*, St. Ciaran's Mount. Coupled with the winding lanes of the Curraghs it is one of the best places to tour. The drive starts on Ramsey Promenade but before setting off be sure to take in the lovely sight of the bay and the slopes of *Liargee Frissel*, Frissel's slope – it's the hill with the tower set on the summit.

Driving along the Mooragh Promenade gives you a feeling of a bygone age when there was time aplenty. You may even be rewarded with a glimpse of St. Bee's Head in Cumberland, the nearest point any of the adjacent islands come to the Isle of Man. At the end of the Promenade bear left up the hill and join the A10 just alongside the excellent Grand Island Hotel. Follow this road to the lovely village of Bride. The church acts as a good landmark for miles around, so if you feel the need for a little guidance, keep your eyes on the spire, it is easy to lose one's bearings in the far North. At Bride take the A16 marked for the Point of Ayre. Again it is an easy place to find because the lighthouse stands as a sentinel for sailors and landlubbers alike. Built in the early years of last century, it reminds all avid readers of adventure stories that Robert Louis Stevenson's great-grandfather was the builder. Definitely not the place to go swimming, the waters surrounding the Point are some of the most treacherous in the world.

On now to the Lhen, so reverse the route back as far as Bride and turn right and West at the church. Lovely country here with good farming land rolling down to the coast. Stay on the A10 and the Lhen is reached after a pleasant drive of a few miles. Watch

TOUR 3

Bride

Days Out by Car

View from Jurby Church

out for the sharp turn at the Lhen Bridge. If you are fond of beach picnics then the little park close to the shore is ideal – but don't lose your car keys, especially if it's a Mylchreests car – it is a long way to a garage! Just a couple of miles further on, is Jurby. This village long ago was an important area for the Vikings and although it has lost something of its old eminence it is nonetheless a pleasant part of our land and well worth exploring for its beaches, church and crosses. Carrying on still further on the A10 we are on the look out for The Cronk, The Hill, such as it is. Go straight on here at the crossroads following the B9 and turn left at the second road down from *The Cronk* crossroads... don't count any farm tracks or lanes. If you have got it right, it should be the yellow coloured road on the map taking you towards *Dollagh Mooar,* Black Lake and the *Curraghs,* Mire or Marsh. Caution here because the roads are extremely narrow and there are lots of ditches awaiting the careless driver. Cross the A14, approximately half way between Sandygate to the North and Sulby to the South – and you are still following the yellow road to Kella and West Sulby.

Turn left at the junction and for a brief distance you are on the TT course on the famous Sulby Straight A3. Just past Sulby Bridge is the Ginger Hall public house and you should turn right here onto the B8 which will fetch you onto the *Sulby Claddaghs,* the River Meadowland. The Claddaghs hold affectionate memories for generations of the Manx, happy reminders of family and Sunday School picnics, camping and more. Leaving memories and picnics behind, we move through the Claddaghs to the A14 or the Sulby Glen Road and begin the ascent of the glen towards Tholt-e-Will. This extremely scenic route brings you up past the Sulby Reservoir built in the early eighties with an eye to securing our water supplies well into the next century. Watch out for sheep on this road, they are not always party to the good custom and practice of the Highway Code. The upper reaches of the road rolls across the shoulder of Snaefell and the scenery is typical of high moorland interspersed with plantation.

The end of the A14 joins the A18 TT course at the Bungalow. There is an Electric Railway station here and during the season the Snaefell Mountain Railway operates regular services between Snaefell summit

and Laxey far below at the bottom of the valley. Turn left and travel the "wrong way" around the TT course, it is still a fast stretch of road and in high winds or misty conditions it is a place to be avoided. The bonus of the road is to be found in clear weather, summer or winter, with fine views of the Ayres, Scotland, England and Ireland. Please take care on the final descent into Ramsey, there are some sharp corners. Once into Royal Ramsey the final destination is yours, it is an easy town to find your way about and the A18 takes the driver right into Parliament Square. Turn right just through the Square and you are into Derby Road and West Quay. Cross the Swing Bridge and the Mooragh Promenade awaits.

Left: Sulby Reservoir
Below: View from the A18 towards Ramsey

MYLCHREESTS DRIVE 4

Peel: St. John's: Cronk-y-Voddy: West Baldwin: Ballasalla: Castletown: Foxdale

Miles 40

Peel is a must for all visitors and if you are not actually staying there then an early visit should be a high priority. Mylchreests Drive 4 will take you from Peel through the Island's lovely hinterland, taking in moorland, valleys and glens. We take as our starting point the north end of Peel Promenade in the vicinity of the Empire Garage and proceed up Stanley Road turning right then almost immediately left into Church Street. At the halt sign – you will observe Peel Police station across the road – take a left and head into Derby Road and the A20 signposted for St. John's. You will know that you have the right road when you pass the Poortown quarry and after about a mile and a half turn right down the small road marked Tynwald Mills. This is a development that the Isle of Man can consider justifiably to be one of the jewels in the crown and it is well worth allowing plenty of time for a stop here.

Leave the Tynwald Mills complex by the opposite end and bear left onto the TT course, the A3. Warning! The exit onto the main road is narrow and sometimes approaching cars from your right hand side may be travelling at speed. Now you are heading up the beautiful wooded Glen Helen road and if you still feel like stretching your legs, stop awhile and stroll up the glen. From opposite the glen car park the road climbs steeply for a short distance passing the famous TT landmark Sarah's Cottage, on up *Creg Willeys Hill*, Willy Syl's or Sylvester's Crag and on to *Cronk-y-Voddy*, which translated from the Manx means the Hill of the Dog. Here at the crossroads we turn right and leave civilisation behind for a little while as we head up hill and down dale to Little London. No big city traffic problems here, but do watch out for approaching traffic as it is only a minor road.

Little London long ago was famous for fishing but nowadays its peace and tranquillity is only disturbed by the occasional passing car, or the rambler who braves the strenuous hill walks and almost stumbles

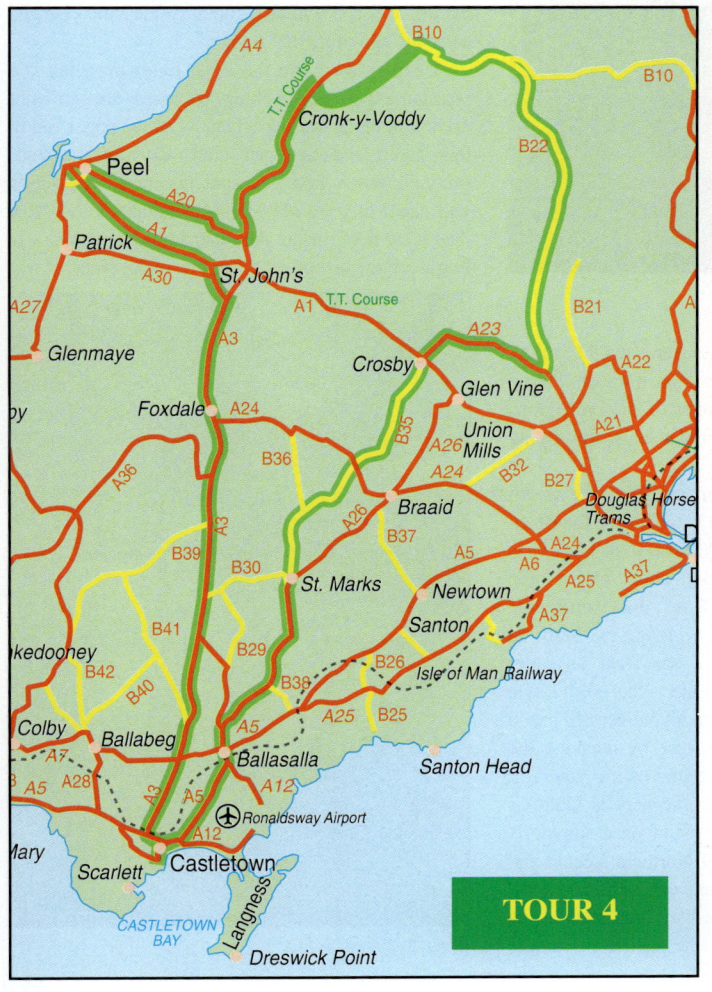

Peel

of the Mountains of Mourne and the Mull of Galloway. You are now heading along the Brandywell Road with Colden Mountain ahead and to the right. There are a lot of cattle grids in the mountains so be sure to take care crossing them and if you have to use the gates, please don't forget to close them after use. Keep a look out for the B22 turning; it should be easy to spot because it is just before Brandywell Cottage, and that is the only building on the left since you started on the B10. Turn off to the right and head along the Injebreck Road, and if you want a good idea of what the centre of the Island looks like, pull in just before the crest of the hill and you will see a countryside little changed since the end of the Ice Age.

Heading down into the West Baldwin valley is a pleasant experience evoking, for many, memories of driving in the Scottish Highlands. At the upper end of this green and treelined cleft, *Carraghan* stands sentinel. When first you spot this peak, realisation will dawn that the old Manx inhabitants knew what they were doing when they named the mountain – in English it means rough, craggy or rocky place. It was

on it by chance. Before the last war, the Old Smithy was the home of the famous flyer Captain Pixton who was the first British winner of the prestigious Schneider Trophy and the holder of many flying records.

The road out of Little London skirts the South West slopes of *Sartfell*, which is old Norse for Black Mountain or Dark Slope. In Manx it is known as *Slieau Dhoo* and joins the B10 about half a mile above *Barregarrow,* Rough Road. Just before the minor road joins the main road is Sartfield Farmhouse Restaurant. If you are from an older generation you will remember the old style farmhouse food, if you are from a younger age group then you will have nothing to lose by breaking the journey at this delightful place and eating your fill. At anytime of day or night the scenery is fabulous and from this unique vantage point on a summer's eve the flashing lighthouses of Northern Ireland and the Mull of Galloway in Scotland can clearly be seen.

Turn up the hill and on the way look back at the view; on clear days there are fine panoramic images

River Neb – St. Johns

Castletown

Colby Glen

chosen as an ideal spot for the Injebreck Reservoir which has served Douglas and much of the Island for many decades. On down the valley, keep to the B22 all the way until Mount Rule halt sign, where a right turn puts the motorist onto the A23 bound for the central village of Crosby. Hard to imagine that the road you are following would, in an era of long ago, have been edging along the South coast of the larger of the two northern islands that made up the Isle of Man at the time of the last Ice Age.

Straight across the *Crosby* crossroads and up the B35 towards St Mark's. It is likely that at one time a cross stood somewhere near the site of the present day village, because its name is derived from the Scandinavian word for Cross Village or Farm. The Mylchreests route is now taking you on one of the drivable parts of the Millenium Way. In 1979 the Manx Nation gave itself a present to commemorate 1,000 years of unbroken parliamentary rule and if you feel that you have not yet really stretched your legs since arriving on our shores... then try walking the full distance, it's only twenty eight miles!

St Mark's is a quiet little backwater and lies peacefully on a rise, giving it the status of a landmark for ramblers, cyclists and motorists alike, visible for a good distance around the parish of Malew. Once a year it comes to life with the holding of the ancient St Mark's Fair. A couple of miles or so further on you come to the busy village of Ballasalla. In more recent times there has been an upsurge in commercial activities here and the little village school does sterling work in preparing the children for senior school and life in the outside world. There is plenty to do in Ballasalla and if you are hungry by now, there are no better places to eat your fill than by visiting La Rosette or The Bistro, two of the finest award winning eating houses in the Isle of Man. If you have children in the car take a diversion just as you are coming into Ballasalla and enjoy the delights of Silverdale Glen – it is well signposted.

As you come into the centre of the village there are a couple of roundabouts to circumnavigate, but take care as there can be exciting moments experienced on them. Driving directions require you to go straight on at each roundabout looking for the Airport and Castletown signs, the A5. Pass the Airport on your left and drive into Castletown. The old Capital is described in detail elsewhere and it is well worth planning a prolonged visit. This is a disc parking area so don't forget to place it in a clear position on the dashboard.

The journey back to Peel is fairly straight forward. Retrace the route back along the harbour to Victoria Road and the first roundabout, where you should turn left into Alexander Road, crossing over the Alexander Bridge. Carry on for a quarter of a mile and turn right into Malew Road and the A3. Stay on the A3, climbing up the Ballamodha Straight before dropping down through the mining villages of Upper and Lower Foxdale. Approaching St John's the road divides at a small hamlet called The Hope – don't worry it is not shown on many maps – take the left branch and follow the A30 past the Forestry Board's nurseries until you reach the halt sign. A good guide if you are on the correct route is that Tynwald Hill is across the road. Turn left for Peel and follow the A1 and the signs all the way to Peel Promenade and the end of Drive 4.

MYLCHREESTS DRIVE 5

Port Erin: The Slogh: Niarbyl: Glen Maye: Foxdale: Braaid: Union Mills: Douglas: Ballasalla: Port St. Mary: Cregneash

Miles 42

Port Erin is a good place to base yourself for a motoring holiday, be it with your own vehicle or a Mylchreests hire car. Parking is easy and although parts of the village are disc zones, they present no real difficulties to the visitor. This drive is started on the Upper Promenade in the vicinity of one of the Port Erin Group of hotels and will cover the southern portion of the Island. It is a journey that will take you from the steep cliffs and hills of the South West, through the gentle rolling hills of Glenfaba, Rushen and Middle Sheadings to the Capital, and on to the old Manx hill village of Cregneash.

Drive up the hill away from the hotels and look for the signposts to Bradda. The village nestles on the slopes of Bradda Head and is divided into West and East, although the exact boundary between them is now somewhat blurred. This is the A32 and it brings you along a gradually widening road to *Ballafesson,* which appears on the ancient manorial roll as MacPherson's Farm. At the junction we pick up the A7 for a short while and at the next crossroads – marked as a roundabout – we turn left on the A36, up through *Ballakillowey,* McGillowey's Farm. It should be noted that the Manx usually exchanged the prefix Mac for the prefix Balla as far as place names were concerned. Just before the junction with the B44 is reached, there is a nice open picnic area.

If it is not too early for a rest, stop here, have a flask of coffee or tea, drink in the views over Castletown Bay, and take in the sweep of the coast right round to The Howe and Cregneash. These are the ancestral lands of the writer's wife and as such remain a firm favourite for the views and the history of the area. Driving on ever upwards on this the Slogh Road, the driver and passengers are continually rewarded with different aspects of this particularly fine landscape around almost every corner. There are many fine walks and for the less energetic, there can hardly be any better places on the Island for picnics. It is an area that probably satisfies the argument as to whether a car is needed

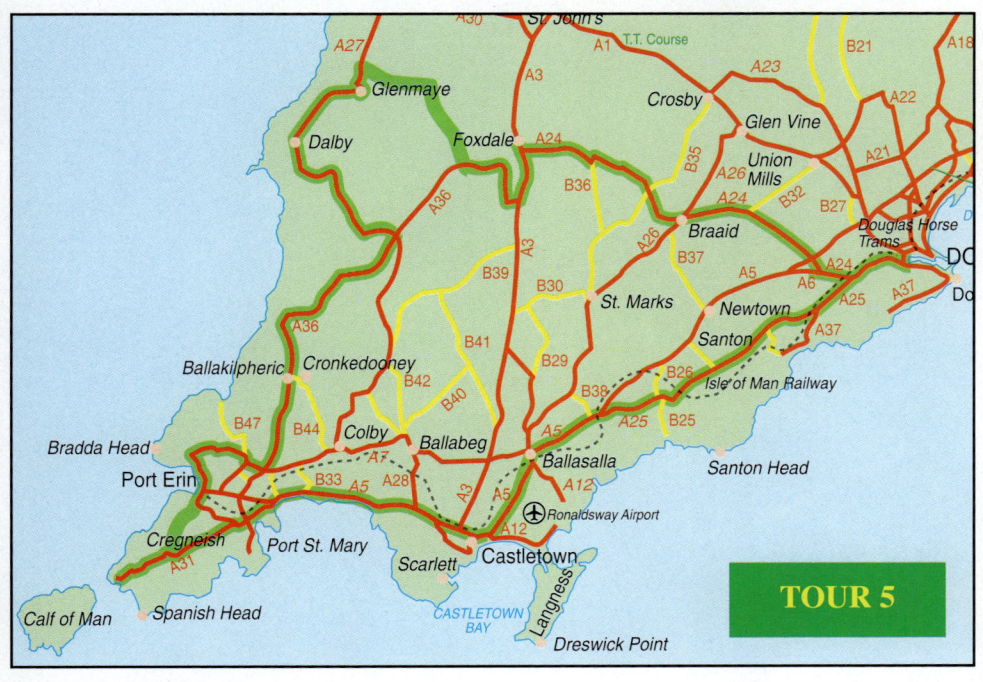

Eairy Dam – Foxdale

Calf Sound

on a visit to Ellan Vannin. Even on a short visit, it is well worth hiring a Mylchreets car just to take in the views you can witness on this particular drive.

The Slogh Road takes you to the Round Table crossroads, shades of King Arthur here? Indeed not so very long ago, a famous American academic proved to a lot of people's satisfaction that this sixth century legendary British king and Camelot were as one with the Isle of Man. Who knows for sure, but little of the area has changed in the intervening centuries and with just a tiny bit of imagination ...! Turn sharp left here onto the A27 and down to *Niarbyl*. Descending the hill into Dalby village, it is easy to see whence the name for Niarbyl is derived. Jutting out into the clear waters of the Irish Sea is a tail of rocks and that is precisely how Niarbyl translates into English. If you have stopped at the nearby Ballacallin Hotel for lunch, then it may be helpful to walk your meal off by enjoying a visit to Niarbyl. Take the minor road down to the shore and while away the time on the rocky beach at the foot of the cliffs.

From Dalby the A27 continues on to *Glen Maye*, loosely translated meaning Yellow Glen on account of the muddy, almost clay coloured waters of the streams running down the glen. If time permits, there are a number of easy walks here, but if it is on you want to go, then proceed to the village post office. To the side of the building there is a narrow country lane which takes you up towards *Garey*, rough or rugged river-shrubbery. Care is needed when traversing this road. Up here on the high ground, if there ever was a river, it has long since disappeared! Perhaps the road was the river because in wet winter weather, the road does seem to double as a stream. There is another name for this road, the Back of the Moon Road and as it is a lonely place, be sure you have plenty of fuel. Rushen Mines soon loom up and even the isolation of the mines have a particular beauty of their own. Back onto the A36 with a left turn and down the mountain to South Barrule Plantation and the junction with the A3. Head left towards Foxdale where you take the first right and join the A24. Skirt the edge of the Eairy Dam – watch out for the ducks crossing the road – and on to *The Braaid*, literally translated it means throat or windpipe as applied in the sense of a glen or sheltered vale. This tiny collection of houses plays host to a favourite beauty spot for locals and visitors alike. Proceed straight on at the roundabout, head up the hill about half a mile, and look down and across into the central valley. The view here is known as the Plains of Heaven... enjoy it!

Carry on this road until you arrive at a major road junction where the A24 bisects the A5, cross over and drive to *Kewaigue,* which translates into Little Hollow. If you would like to re-visit Douglas, continue on into town, if not then just past the new Isle of Man Breweries headquarters, turn through an acute right hander and head for Santon on the A25. *Santon* – in older times it was spelt Santan – derives its name from Saint Sanctan but further identification of this saintly figure and his "living" has proved difficult for the modern scholar. This road is known as the Old Castletown Road and there are a number of roads leading off it down to rocky bays and isolated coves. Try them when you have time, most are off the beaten track and are not accessible by public transport. The road takes you in the direction of Ballasalla and rejoins the A5 at a spot where the railway line passes under the main road. Stay on the A5 by turning left at the Ballasalla roundabout – the Whitestone Inn faces you directly ahead as you approach it. Leave Castletown behind by using the bypass, it's still the A5, drive along the edge of *Bay ny Carrickey,* The Bay of the Rock, and turn right up past the tall stone building along Beach Road, heading for the crossroads, where you go straight on using the A31. Ignore any other roads and make for Cregneash. Plenty to see here, and when you have had your fill, carry on down to The Calf Sound to enjoy the totally unspoiled scenery of the Isle of Man's equivalent of Lands End.

The final stages of the drive see us returning back up the hill from The Sound towards Cregneash again. Just before entering the village from the South, turn sharp left onto the minor road leading past Mull Hill and its stone circles. Dating from Neolithic times, this unspoilt area remains much as the earliest inhabitants would have known it. Almost home, but take care, this is a single track road with passing places. Port Erin nestles quietly below as you drive down Dandy Hill and onto the Lower Promenade.

Plains of Heaven

MYLCHREESTS DRIVE 6

Onchan: Baldrine: Laxey: Glen Roy: The Bungalow: Sulby: St. Judes: Andreas: Bride: Ramsey: The Gooseneck: The Hibernian: Dhoon: Laxey

Miles 49

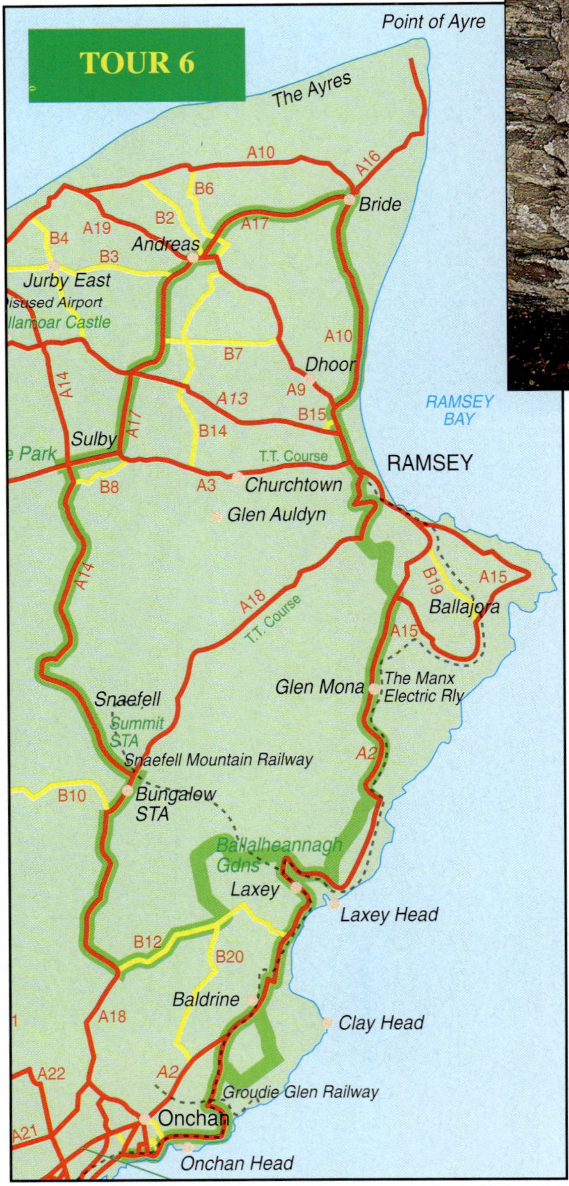

Manx milestone

Onchan started life as a small village to the North of Douglas and has in recent times seen a growth outstripping that of the modern day capital. Unsuspecting souls could almost be forgiven for thinking that it is a suburb of Douglas, but the good citizens of the village have their own local government and are intensely proud of their separate existence.

We will start our drive at Onchan Head, just above Port Jack. Follow the A11 as it runs parallel to the tram track, passing as you go Groudle Glen. There is a minor road off to the right, approximately half a mile past Groudle Station and a detour up this road will bring the motorist to Old Kirk Lonan Church, well worth a visit. Completing the detour brings you out onto the A2 just to the South of Baldrine village. Carry on towards Laxey via Fairy Cottage and Old Laxey Hill – bear to the right at the Filling Station – and the quaint harbour awaits you.

Laxey owes its origins to the Norsemen

Laxey Station

TT road sign

who named it Salmon River. Give yourself time here or, at the very least, a promise to return for a longer visit. From the harbour travel up the glen and when you reach the woollen mills, go up the hill, under the railway bridge and straight on at the stop sign looking for the Creg-ny-Baa signpost. You are now on the Glen Roy Road (coloured yellow on the OS map) and about to experience one of the best glen drives on the Island. The glen was formed by the waters cascading down from *Mullagh Ouyr, Slieau Meayll,* Dun Summit, Bare or Bald Mountain and Windy Corner respectively. Care on this road is required as there are a number of blind corners, and the road is extremely narrow in places. Eventually you rejoin a wider road, the B12 just above Social Cottage, and by turning in a South West (right) direction, the road brings you to the well known Keppel Hotel at Creg-ny-Baa. Turn right and head the "wrong way" round the TT course, the A18, aiming for the Bungalow. Just past Brandywell is the highest point on the course at almost 1,400 feet above sea level.

The Bungalow actually bears no resemblance to a

modern building of that name and the current site was home, until fairly recently, to a magnificent hotel made of wood and galvanised sheeting – very popular with TT fans. Watch out for the directions to Sulby and turn left on the A14. If your companions fancy some fresh air, pull up at the top entrance to *Tholt-e-Will* Glen. Give them half an hour or so to walk the glen and pick them up just outside the inn at the bottom of the hill. However if a picnic is the order of the day then drive into the Sulby Reservoir car park and you will not be disappointed with the views. The name of the glen translated from the Manx means Hill of the Cattlefold, and the inhabitants of the lower end of the bigger glen have traditionally been known as the Sulby Cossacks. At any time of the year, Sulby Glen has a beauty all of its own. In the spring the East side of the glen colours itself with a blue haze as the bluebells fight each other for space. At other times the heather and gorse lend their own particular splash of colour and always the light creates a special atmosphere.

A quarter of the way down the glen from the inn lies Irishman's Cottage and, high above the nearby waterworks, is the small feeder reservoir of *Block Eary*. The reservoir was built up in modern times by German POW's and although it is a strenuous walk, those who partake will be rewarded with a sense of achievement. The name has changed somewhat from the original Scandinavian spelling *Blakkarg* but the meaning is still the same, Black Sheiling, from the peaty colour of the stream.

Proceed on down the valley towards the Sulby Straight. If you feel the need for some refreshment the Peppermill Restaurant at Sulby Mill comes recommended. Carl and his hardworking staff are open seven nights a week during the summer months,

and they will see you well fed for the next stage of your drive. From the Sulby Mill go straight on to the main road and turn right onto the TT Course at Sulby Methodist Church. At the end of the Straight turn off the A3 onto the St Judes Road, the A17. From the West Craig crossroads stay on the A17 to Andreas. There is a subtle change in the scenery here as the land changes from moor and glen to low lying, well drained marsh land.

Andreas has a fine church dedicated to Saint Andrew from whom the parish takes its name. The village is very much the centre of local agricultural activities. Leave Andreas by continuing on the same road which takes you to the Island's northern most centre of population, Bride. The village lies in a little hollow of the Bride Hills and is one of the sunniest places on the Isle of Man according to the local meteorological office.

Leaving Bride behind us, we move along the A10 in the direction of Ramsey and if you are in need of a refreshment break then you could do no better than to call into the Grand Island Hotel which can cater for most tastes. The Bride road takes you right into Parliament Square and if you are not breaking your journey in Ramsey, a town which is highly recommended, then carry on following the route marked for the TT Course. High above the town at the Gooseneck there is a minor road leading off behind the marshals' shelter. Careful negotiation of the turn is required to get onto what is known as the Hibernian Road. This is a delightful run across the lower slopes of *North Barrule* and whilst there seems to be no trace of the name's origination, it is most likely that it takes its form from the same meaning as *South Barrule,* Ward Mountain, a name which has close connections with the ancient system of "Watch and Ward."

As you come off this road at the Hibernian, turn right onto the A2, the Coast Road, and head for the Corrany. This name is a variation of *Cornaa* which means Treen, the modern version of homestead. At the *Dhoon,* Fort Quarterland, and probably taking its name from the nearby earthworks of *Kionehenin,* The Head of the Precipice, you can always stop and let your passengers return by tram to Onchan. So your Mylchreests car and the dedicated drives are hopefully going to prove useful in more ways than

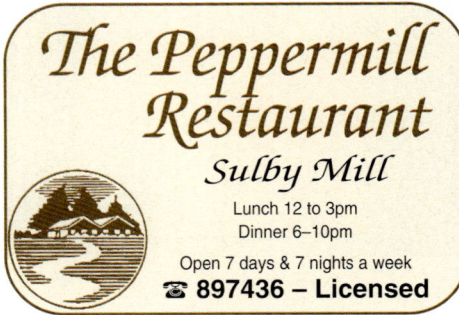

The Peppermill Restaurant
Sulby Mill
Lunch 12 to 3pm
Dinner 6–10pm
Open 7 days & 7 nights a week
☎ 897436 – Licensed

Sulby

Douglas Bay

one. Leave the Dhoon car park area by the B11, the *Ballaragh Road*. This is an interesting name and although its derivation is doubtful, there is reason to believe that perhaps its original meaning was Farm of the Spectre or Apparition. Just before the end of this road, King Orry's Grave is reached.

Turn right here and you are once again back on the A2. At Laxey, turn over the tram lines into Dumbell's Terrace, known to the locals as Ham and Egg Terrace, and park the car. Looking up the valley, your gaze rests upon the largest working water wheel in the world, Lady Isabella. For the less energetic or the elderly, you can in fact carry on up the valley to a car park which is adjacent to the Wheel.

The final leg of your journey takes you from Laxey along the A2 to just South of Baldrine village where you veer left after the tram level crossing lights onto the A11, Groudle Road. It is worth noting that trams do travel in both directions and the unwary motorist can be caught out at this crossing. Passing through Groudle you may catch sight of the popular Groudle miniature railway as it chugs around the headland. Soon the road grants you a fine view of Douglas Bay and then Port Jack is in sight.

CAR RENTAL
FROM £99

0624 823533

MYLCHREESTS
CAR RENTAL

YOU CAN'T BEAT MYLCHREESTS

Rent a car from Mylchreests and you'll drive a great deal.
Our weekly rentals start as little as 399 including insurance and VAT.
A weekend rental costs from only £69 including insurance and VAT.
**All cars have radios
Maps and Tourist information with all cars
24 hour vehicle assistance service
Free baby & child seats
Special discounts for payment in advance**
For full details of our car rentals and special offers call us today - you'll find us hard to beat
All offers subject to availability

GETTING AROUND THE ISLAND

As the title suggests, this section of the guide deals with the internal transport system of the Isle of Man… or you could walk! Nowhere on the Island is geographically more than five and a half miles from the sea and the many roads and tracks criss-crossing the countryside soon bring you back to the coast. The walkers amongst the readers may well be interested to learn that the Manxman calls his walking-stick *Bock-Yaun-Fannee*, John the Flayer's Pony. So named because John was said to have flayed his poor beast and to have as a consequence been obliged to travel on foot.

There are good maps of the Isle of Man available and if you are a keen rambler then a good buy is the Isle of Man Public Rights of Way Map, which is published by the Isle of Man Department of Highways, Ports and Properties. The OS Map has been referred to elsewhere in the publication and is an excellent guide to people as they move around the Island. The Island measures at its extremities 33 miles (52kms) by 13 miles (22kms) and with a total land mass area of some 227 square miles (572 sq.kms) there is a large area to explore.

Disembarking from the ferry at Douglas, you are transported back into a bygone age. In transport terms the Isle of Man lies in a time warp, where even the surrounding Irish Sea seems little changed. Life is mush as we imagined it was on the adjacent islands decades ago. Running the length of the Douglas Promenades, in front of the brightly painted hotels and guesthouses, the echoing clip-clop of the horse trams immediately relaxes the tourists and is a reminder of pre motor vehicle days. Dating from 1876, the horse trams offer a leisurely trot between the Jubilee Clock to the Strathallan Terminus at Summerland. There are numerous tram stops, but please take care when boarding or alighting from the trams… and do pay attention to the instructions from the conductors. The open air trams are known as "toast racks", look at the first one you see and you will understand why! Don't worry about the horses, all 40 plus animals are specially trained for the traffic and the track is so designed that a man can actually pull, with

Douglas Station

JOHN HENDY

TRAVEL BACK IN TIME

Discover the Isle of Man with Isle of Man Transport. The Victorian Manx Electric Railway, Snaefell Mountain Railway and Steam Railway offer a unique way to enjoy the Island in a relaxed and leisurely fashion.

The Snaefell Mountain Railway celebrates its centenary in 1995 with many special events on offer.

Let Isle of Man Transport chauffeur you around our Island. The Isle of Man also has a well integrated bus network so making just about every part of the island accessible.

Special Island Freedom tickets offer a variety of ways to enjoy the Island's natural beauty, villages, towns and a wealth of visitor attractions.

Isle of Man transport
Strathallan Crescent
Douglas, Isle of Man IM2 4NR

TRAIN & BUS ENQUIRIES 0624 663366

Snaefell Railway

ease, a fully laden tram along the full length of the route. The working conditions are good with short days – a two hour shift per day in the season and all winter off to enjoy the grazing – and that just for the horses!

Douglas Corporation operates a pension scheme for these delightful beasts of burden and when the time comes to retire a permanent home awaits them at the Isle of Man Home of Rest for Old Horses. If you love horses take a trip out to the Home of Rest on Richmond Hill, it's on the bus route to Castletown with a stop right outside and there is ample parking for cars by the stables. Take care here when turning or crossing the road because the premises are on a fast stretch of main road. A firm favourite with all, the horses love to see the visitors and usually respond when called by name.

Strathallan Terminus at the North end of the bay, houses the rolling stock and provides workshop facilities for the Manx Electric Railway. In 1993 the MER celebrated its centenary. These are no replicas but the original rolling stock from the 1890s, and passengers are offered a genuine opportunity to step back in time and experience this working "time capsule". If you are fortunate you may be on board one of two of the oldest working tramcars still in use anywhere in the world, and travel to Ramsey along the twisting and turning seventeen and a half mile route to Ramsey via the important railhead in the village of Laxey. There you will find the only mixed gauge railway junction in the British Isles from where you can switch to the Snaefell Mountain Railway, the only electrically worked mountain railway still operating in the British Isles.

Change systems at Laxey for the four mile climb to the summit of the Island's highest point... it's a must for all visitors. The slow and gradual ascent up the side of Laxey Glen provides bird's eye views of the famous Laxey Wheel, restored and acting as a reminder that not so many decades ago Laxey was a centre for lead and zinc mining. After crossing the TT Course, the trams pause for a short while at the Bungalow Station before tackling the final stretch to the summit of *Snaefell*. The Summit Station and cafe is the work place of the "highest paid person" on the Island. A short walk brings you to the mountain's peak. Catch your breath and take in the seven Kingdoms, the trip is worth it just for that view alone. After enjoying such inspiring views, the return journey awaits. Descending the mountain can leave you almost with a sense of loss. In no time at all the Snaefell tram is soon passing above the outlying houses and Dumbell's Terrace – former homes of the brave miners.

From Laxey, many tourists retrace their journey to Douglas past pretty little stations rejoicing in wonderful names such as Fairy Cottage, Ballabeg, Baldrine, Groudle Glen and Onchan. Others head North via the stations of Cornaa, Ballajora and Dreemskerry to Ramsey. To commemorate the MER's centenary a new visitor centre has been opened at the northern terminus. Open during the season it is dedicated to the fascinating history of the railway. Ramsey played its part in the building of the Mountain Railway, for it was from there that in 1895 the ten year old steam engine "Caledonia" was sent by sea to Laxey. After careening the vessel in Laxey harbour the engine was moved on baulks and rollers through the village to the station to assist in the construction of the new railway. What a feat the building of the railway must have been and what a contribution from the "Caledonia". Steaming up and down the mountain daily without the benefit of fell brakes this, the heaviest engine in Manx railway history did the job on the hand and steam brakes alone.

Getting Around the Island 139

Laxey

In June 1872 on the waste land of South Douglas known locally as "The Lake", a gang of navvies began work on what was to become a railway terminus. At the top end of Douglas inner harbour is a rather imposing red brick building now doing service as the Island's Customs and Excise Service headquarters but which originally was the headquarters of the Railway Company.

The Isle of Man Steam Railway is one of the Island's unique institutions, protected by Government, the public and by a work force that has a fierce pride and a dedication much envied by larger systems elsewhere. From Douglas Station the one hundred and twenty year old rolling stock carries you along in a pleasant bumping and rolling fashion to Port Erin in the far South of the Island, along sixteen miles of well maitained track. On past Ballasalla, historical Castletown and Port St Mary to the centre of the South West village of Port Erin, the track wends its busy way. There is usually time to have a look around the near vicinity of the railhead and if your hobby is trains the Railway Museum is certainly worth a visit. The railway cafe is recommended for a cup of tea or some home made cakes or scones. The Station's waiting rooms are full of railway memorabilia, evoking memories of another era, long lost to many places in the British Isles... ah happy days!

The Douglas – Port Erin line is all that remains to remind the visitor of a network of steam railways which also took the traveller from the capital to Peel and Ramsey via the Island's central valley. The northern line branched off at St John's. Great was the excitement generated when the Peel and Ramsey trains left St John's Station simultaneously and appeared to race for the "right of track". In reality there were of course two tracks, but it used to amuse the passengers and was a throw back to the days when two separate railway companies operated to Peel and Ramsey. From St John's, a railway line was laid up the glen to link Foxdale lead mines with the main line system. The ardent railway enthusiast will soon find that there were many more railways on the Island and there is a lot of fun to be had searching for old tracks and buildings.

Trains, trams or cars are not the only way of seeing the Island. Isle of Man Transport, which is a Division of the Department of Tourism, Leisure and Transport operates an Island wide bus service. Careful study of their timetables will show the tourist that bus times are usually carefully integrated where possible with the trains and trams. The fun of roaming the countryside by bus is that one gets an opportunity to have a "skeet" over the hedge as you journey along.

Privately owned coaches also operate on the Island. The most popular of the companies is Tours Isle of Man, offering morning, afternoon and evening mystery tours or full day round the Island tours as well as providing transfer services for package holidays from and to the Sea and Air Terminals. Their blue and white liveried vehicles depart from bases on Douglas Promenade throughout the season and a trip out on one of their coaches is worthwhile. Tours drivers have an encyclopaedic knowledge of the Isle of Man and are always glad to lend a helping hand when needed. Not content with driving around the Island, they also operate a comprehensive holiday tour programme to the UK, Ireland and Europe, so there is a lot of experience behind the wheel and in dealing with the travelling public.

Hire and Drive vehicles are an extremely popular means of getting around the Island. First amongst the companies is Mylchreests. Hiring a modern car from Mylchreests gives you quality of service and the freedom to come and go as you please. The friendly folk in the hire department are pleased to help in any way they can and should you require a baby/child seat this can be supplied... and there is no charge. But please try and give them a little bit of advance notice and an idea of the children's ages. Arrangements can be made to meet you at the Sea Terminal or pick you up from your hotel or accommodation, and their Airport Office is open for all confirmed arrivals. If you need advice on getting around the Island ask Mylchreests, there is no one who knows the roads of Mann better than them. The service also includes a free Isle of Man Map and a map of Douglas.

There is a good range of cars in the Mylchreests fleet to suit most tastes and pockets, and there are a number of choices relating to hire periods. If you don't need a car for the whole of your stay then ask about the special Weekenders or Week Specials. Phil Carr (he is the boss) and the team will gladly tailor a package to suit you, and by the way ask them about the Isle of Man's Magnetic Hill, it's fun with a car! To help you gain the maximum pleasure from your visit, Mylchreests offer you a variety of pre-planned drives which are described elsewhere in this guide.

The Isle of Man's unique transport system allows the visitor to travel easily around the Island. For many people it is the main reason for visiting, others see it as an unexpected bonus but whatever the reason this is no modern day replica of how things used to be. The engines, trams and rolling stock are the originals! They have survived in their original form largely because as a small island, without a huge supporting population they had to last. There never ever was going to be a modernisation or replacement programme, simply because the money was never available and they survived until such time when it was realised that these Victorian modes of transport remained, unharmed by the progress of the twentieth century. The Island's transport system appeals to all ages. It is the means of travelling back to the past without leaving the present; how Jules Verne would have envied us, even if the travel is to the past and not the future! The Isle of Man can offer the visitor an opportunity to leave behind the cares and worries of the modern world even if it only for a short while.

MUSEUMS OF MANN

The early days of the Isle of Man are briefly described elsewhere within this publication, but for the visitor with more than a little passing interest in the Island and its rich history, The Story of Mann really begins with Manx National Heritage, *Eiraght Ashoonagh Vannin*.

Over the centuries the history of Mann has been likened to a tapestry, with people and events drawn together as if colourful threads, creating an image of island life as it was for our forbears. It is a history that tells of great tragedies, great happenings, arts, crafts... and also periods of great happiness. The first-time visitor to our shores soon discerns that history lies around almost every corner and the skillful manner in which Manx National Heritage interprets this tapestry ensures that locals and tourists alike are aware of the value of the past.

The secret of Manx National Heritage's success has been to treat all the heritage sites and the landscape as equals, binding them all together as it were, as one. This innovative idea was rewarded by their being acknowledged as the British Isles Museum of the Year 1992/93. Future planned developments will ensure that the Isle of Man and its heritage will continue to enrich the life of the Island and maintain the lead that the Heritage team give to the adjacent islands and elsewhere. You are invited to turn the pages of our history by visiting as many of the sites as possible.

The Museum is the hub of the many spokes that make up and tell the Story of Mann and whilst the manner of the interpretation is comprehensive, there is no substitution for a visit to the many sites of archaeological and historical importance that abound. There are a number of very good leaflets which give guidance to the various locations and the highly visible road signs ensure that directions are easily followed. If you need a snack, a number of the heritage sites have facilities to cater for most tastes.

Contained within the Island's 227 square miles are prehistoric monuments, Iron Age hill forts, early Christian chapels, Norse houses, collections of ancient crosses and the outstanding Peel and Rushen castles. Moving to more modern eras, there is Tynwald Hill, Cregneash Village, Laxey Wheel, the Nautical Museum, the Grove Museum and much more to visit. All have one thing in common – they blend in with their natural surroundings. Under the Manx National Heritage umbrella, which is well supported by a number of voluntary groups, lies responsibility for the preservation of the Manx countryside. Building developments are required to be sympathetic to the area and the Island as a whole. The extensive land holdings of the Manx National Trust ensure that natural beauty spots are left undisturbed for the enjoyment of the generations to come. The Trust actively encourages the visitor to sample the delights of the unspoilt countryside and this is supplemented by Visitor Centres and Nature Trails.

Travelling around the Island without a car is easy by using the various forms of public transport e.g. the steam and electric railways – working museum pieces in their own right – buses and coaches.

Manx Museum

DISCOVER

The Story of Mann

with the MUSEUM

Manx National Heritage holds the title of 'MUSEUM OF THE YEAR', the highest award for a museum organisation in the British Isles.

'The Story of Mann' begins at the Manx Museum in Douglas, where the latest video technology introduces you to 10,000 years of turbulent Manx history.

The exciting gallery presentations describe 'The Story of Mann' from the time of 'The Great Deer' to the present day, with the Manx Finance Sector and the famous T.T. Races. This is your invitation to discover 'The Story of Mann' throughout one of the most concentrated and best cared for historic landscapes in Europe.

Spectacular displays at Castle Rushen recreate life in the age of 'The Kings and Lords of Mann', while the Great Laxey Wheel tells the story of the 'Laxey Miners'.

At Cregneash Village Folk Museum, a living illustration of a 19th century Manx crofting community, contrasts with the more affluent farming picture at the Grove Museum in Ramsey.

Together with the Nautical Museum and the Old Grammar School; Odin's Raven, and Peel Castle; these heritage sites portray the themes that form part of the unique 'Story of Mann'.

Collect your **"free" Story of Mann** leaflets from your hotel or tourist information centre.

THE MANX MUSEUM, DOUGLAS

SHIPS AND THE SEA • CELTS AND VIKINGS

OF THE YEAR

KINGS AND LORDS OF MANN

Manx National Heritage
Eiraght Ashoonagh Vannin

LAXEY MINERS • FARMERS AND CROFTERS

Bradda Head

Main Holiday Events

MARCH
Isle of Man Open Darts Festival

APRIL
Isle of Man Art Society Exhibition

Easter Festival of Sport and Drama

Student Festival of Sport

MAY
Peel Sports Festival

Transport Enthusiasts Week

Manx National Rally

International Whitsun Hockey Festival

Isle of Man Brass Band Festival

JUNE
TT Festival Motorcycle Practices

TT Festival Motorcycle Race Days

Steam Packet National Road Races, Billown Circuit

Isle of Man Crown Green Bowling Festival

International Cycle Week

Kart Grand Prix, Peel

JULY
Tynwald Day

Maritime Festival

Southern 100 Races, Billown Circuit

Summer Spectacular IOM Railways

International Football Festival

Ramsey Angling Week

AUGUST
Carnival Dance Championships

Mannin Angling Festival

Manx Grand Prix Motorcycle Practice Periods

Manx Two Day Motorcycle Trial

Manx Grand Prix Motorcycle Race Days

SEPTEMBER
Isle of Man Crown Green Bowling Festival

Manx International Car Rally

Manx Classic Car Races

For more information and confirmation of these events please telephone the Tourist Information Centre on 0624 686766 or for general inquiries Isle of Man Department of Tourism on 0624 686801.
Details correct at time of going to press.

LEGENDS OF MANN

Timetables are readily available or ring 663366/ 662525 for up to date travel information. A car is recommended though because some of the smaller heritage sites are off the beaten track.

Without doubt the best place to acquaint yourself with what Manx National Heritage has to offer is to begin by visiting the Manx Museum in Douglas. If you are on foot, head for St Thomas's Church and the Museum lies just behind it, at the top of Crellins Hill. Should you be driving to the Museum there are usually plenty of parking spaces in the Chester Street car park, which is connected to the Museum by a footbridge. For those folk who have a handicapped person in their party, it is possible to pull up outside the main doors and discharge passengers but please note, parking and turning space is very restricted outside the Museum entrance.

The best advice available recommends our visitors start their journey into the past by viewing the magnificent "Story of Mann" film. The atmosphere generated by the film will, it is guaranteed, stay with you for the duration of your visit to the Island. Home to much of the Island's art treasures and artefacts, the Museum is not a place to be rushed. In fact there is no need to even leave it for refreshments as there is an excellent restaurant on site near the well-stocked heritage shop.

For the serious student of history, the modern research facilities offered by the Museum Library are excellent, particularly for delving into family trees. The Island was fortunate in that much of their written records were saved from the worst excesses of Henry VIII and the Reformation.

A helpful note for those visitors who are members of the National Trust, Scottish National Trust, English Heritage and certain overseas trusts, is that admission, on production of the appropriate documentation, is free to all those sites where a charge is normally made.

Enjoy your visit to Manx National Heritage and all it has to offer.

Like many other small communities legends and stories grow up and are perhaps expanded as the years and generations pass by. The Isle of Man is no exception to this generalisation... or is it? You see many of us happen to believe that all the myths, legends and stories handed down to us are true!

Manx place names, as you have seen in other parts of this guide, are different from those in your own locality. The simple explanation could be that in days of yore English was not spoken here hence the lack of English place names and indeed the Manx had to get to grips with the language of the Norsemen. Maybe the landscapes changed, traditions altered or perhaps there was an event of great historical significance, whatever the explanation, there is often no logical reason why a particular place received its name.

Take the name of this fair Isle... you the reader may have always believed its name to be just that, yet the inhabitants know it by several other names. At the time of Caesar in 54 BC the Romans knew it as Mona. A century later the Roman writer and administrator Pliny "The Elder" was calling the Island Monapia. One hundred years on, in 139 AD we find the famous Graeco-Egyptian mathematician and geographer referring to it as Monaoeda. As the centuries rolled by variations of the name surfaced but it is not until the time of the Irish Annals circa 1084-1496 AD that a more recognisable form of our nation's name was seen, Manann or Manand. The rough translation of the name means mountainous or hilly land. There is a school of thought that believes that Mann may have taken its name from Manannan, the Celtic Neptune, God of the Sea, but it is much more likely that he was named from the Island.

For a long time now the Manx have referred to their homeland as Ellan Vannin, though the visitor will still find reference about the Island, to Mann. Whatever your preference please enjoy exploring our Island.

Derbyhaven

The Manx national symbol has for many centuries been the Three Legs of Man. Arguments as to its exact origins have always proved inconclusive but it does seem to have been introduced to the Island at least as long ago as 1266 AD. Alexander III of Scotland adopted the symbol when the Isle of Man was ceded to Scotland. Perhaps his family connections with the Mediterranean island of Sicily holds the answer. In that far off island much use is made of a very similar symbol with the difference being that the Manx legs are armoured, the Sicilian's being bare. Our motto is interesting, *"Quocunque jeceris stabit;* Which ever way you throw me, I shall stand".

If you love wild life then the Island can be paradise. There is a marvellous variety of bird life and the Calf of Man is a world renowned bird sanctuary but don't expect to find any squirrels or snakes. Snakes were allegedly banished by St Maughold when he was thrown from his horse.

Staying on the subject of animals, *Graynoge's* the Manx name for Hedgehogs, it means something causing horror, only came to the Island about 1800. The schooner "Hooton" of Garlieston was wrecked at Rue Point. Amongst the salvage was a box of hedgehogs and some of them made good their escape. In more modern times Wallabies broke free from the Curraghs Wild Life Park and are said to be enjoying "the goodlife" in the North of the Island. The most famous Manx animal resident is the Manx Cat. There are many and varied stories about how they lost their tails... it might be fun for you to find out for yourself!

In Peel Castle under the Keep is a guard-room and it was here that one of the most famous legends in Manx history is set. Each night a large black dog, the *Moddey Dhoo,* would come and lie down in front of the fire. Viewing this apparition by the light of flickering candles the soldiers soon became quite used to its presence although they treated it with the greatest of respect and would not stay in the room alone with it. One day a drunken soldier followed it out of the guardroom, when he returned he was a changed man, and despite much pleading from his friends as to what he had seen died in great agony some three days later.

Dealing with more human creatures takes the visitor to the foot of *Slieau Whallian,* Aleyn's Mountain at St John's, overlooking Tynwald Hill. It was here that tradition has it, that in Viking times witches were punished by being placed into spiked barrels and rolled down the steep slopes of the hill. There is also a tradition that tells of the nearby *Curragh Glass,* Green Marsh, where the accused were put into the water and if they sank were presumed innocent... some good that did them!

Buildings of great age and size are relatively scarce on the Island but they do exist and there are fine examples to be seen in Peel and Rushen castles. Rushen Abbey still has a few buildings standing and there are the remains of over 150 *Keeills,* Churches, dating from the 6th and 7th centuries, dotted about the countryside. Whilst the Island escaped the worst excesses of the Reformation the old buildings acted as stone quarries and suffered accordingly. One building on the Island that is roofless and in good condition is St Trinians Church at Crosby. There has never been a roof on the building, despite three separate attempts to place one on it. Legend tells of a spirit like creature called a Buggane who frightened witless anybody who attempted to roof over the walls.

Near to St Trinian's, legend tells of the Curse of St Patrick, when a thorn ran through his foot as he was in the act of dedicating the Island's first church in 444 AD. His response was to curse the field where the thorn was growing and decree that no crops would grow on this field forever.

On the A5 Douglas to Castletown Road just past Santon Station is the Fairy Bridge. Well sign posted, no self respecting local passes over this bridge without a word of greeting to the "little people". Try *Laa Mie,* Good Day, pronounced "lay my" and they will be pleased! The little people are of course the good fairies.

Manx mythology indicates that there were a number of supernatural beings in existence. The *Phynnodderree,* a Hairy Satyr features often in the legends and seems to have been kindly disposed towards men often using his great strength to their advantage. Warning of future events was given by the Night-man or *Dooiney-oie.* Another friendly spirit and the guardian of certain families was the *Lhiannan Shee.* On the down side was the *Buggane,*

Mauchuld Church

mentioned earlier and very much an evil spirit. The *Cabbyl-Ushtey* was a water-horse, sometimes confused with the *Glashtin,* a Goblin. There also appeared in stories a water-bull, known to the inhabitants of Mann as the *Tarroo-Ushtey.* Much of the legendary history of the Island is recorded in songs and ballads.

The sea has always played an important part in the history of the Island and legends tell of an Irishman, one Buck Whalley who was driven from his native land. To retain his wealth he had to comply with the conditions of his Father's will which required him to always reside on Irish soil. No problem to this enterprising gentleman he simply shipped into the Island several cargoes of Emerald Isle soil and built his house on it. The Fort Anne later became home to Sir William Hilary, founder of the RNLI. The site of this fine building was just above Douglas harbour on Head Road. Unfortunately it has in recent years been demolished.

One of the finest seamen the Island ever produced was Captain Quilliam of H.M.S. Victory fame, but even with his close connections to Nelson he couldn't have had a more direct relationship with the famous hero of Trafalgar than John Lace of Kerrodhoo, Bride. Lace claimed that the shot which fatally wounded the Admiral passed through his arm first. Poor John Lace lost his arm in the incident and later drowned in Ramsey Bay.

The North of the Island seems to have been a good breeding ground for seamen because Sir Baldwin Walker KCB, who was born at Port-e-Vullen, Maughold, managed careers in both the Royal and Turkish Navies. His name when sailing under Turkish colours was Yavir Pasha. Long before Sir George' era it was told that the "Great Harry" built by Henry VIII as the first warship to have guns in her holds, sailed too close to the Manx cliffs and swept several flocks of sheep into the sea with her bowsprit!

A close examination of the Manx Telecom telephone directory reveals that many Manx surnames begin with C, Q, or K. Kerruish is a much respected name in the Island and the legend attached to its origins is fascinating. In the long ago, a ship was wrecked off Maughold and four of the crew were observed swimming for the shore. Because the swimmers were of an undetermined nationality and unable to communicate with the locals they became known as *Kiare Rooisht,* Four Naked. The swimmers settled in Maughold and the name Kerruish is still synonymous with the Sheading.

Stepping ashore again and visiting the Sulby River above Tholt-y-Will, we find a legend telling of a *Tarroo-Ushtey* who lived there. Great care was always taken when travelling in the area. Close by was an old watermill and it is said that every miller who went into this mill disappeared. At last one soul, perhaps braver than the rest decided to solve the mystery. On entering the mill he discovered that a giant had been coming down from the mountain and disposing of the millers. It was "suggested" to the miller by the giant that he would suffer the same fate, but our brave friend volunteered to make himself useful by baking a cake for the giant. Risking his neck, the cunning miller handed the giant a sieve and told him to fetch water for the kneading. Giants are considered to be dull-witted and as he kept repeating the phrase "As fast as I get it, it disappears", the miller made good his escape, the only man to live to tell the tale.

On the subject of giants the largest ever Manxman was James Arthur Caley of Sulby. His full height was seven feet eleven inches and he weighed 44 stones. Arthur lived a relatively short life dying at the age of 43; it is said as a consequence of poisoning by a jealous rival. A cast of one of his hands is on display at the Museum.

There are many other legends told about the life and times of our ancestors. As you explore the Island try and imagine the conditions under which the people lived. It is not too difficult to see how close they lived to nature and how easy it must have been to interpret certain deeds as phenomenons of one kind or another.

HOTELS AND GUESTHOUSES

CASTLETOWN

'FERNLEA', Ballamodha, Nr Ballasalla. Warm friendly welcome, en-suite bedrooms, excellent home cooking, tea/coffee facilities, TV lounge, conservatory, private garden. 10 minutes Airport, 15 minutes Douglas. Picturesque situation, ideal for walking, fishing, bird watching. 2 crowns commended. Tel (0624) 824192.

DOUGLAS

ARRANDALE HOTEL, 39 Hutchinson Square, Douglas. Small, family-run 3 crowns commended hotel situated in quiet residential area of Douglas. Unrestricted street parking. All en-suite rooms have TV, clock/radio, tea/coffee making facilities. Licensed. Tel/Fax (0624) 674907.

ASHTEAD, 9 Christian Road, Douglas. Family run guest house, home cooking, special diets on request. Tea/coffee making facilities. No restrictions. Close to all amenities. Children welcome. Prices from £11 B&B. Proprietor: Jean Twist. Tel (0624) 676790

BROADWAY HOTEL & RESTAURANT, 1 Sherwood Terrace, Broadway, Douglas. Basic accommodation at an affordable price. Bed & breakfast from £10 per person per night. Restaurant open to non residents. Open all year. Sports groups catered for at reduced price. Tel (0624) 675907

CASTLE MONA HOTEL, Central Promenade, Douglas. 28 luxurious bedrooms with private bathrooms, 4 suites with Jacuzzi Bath, 2 with 4 poster beds. Colour TV, satellite, radio, direct-dial telephone, hospitality tray. Restaurant, grand ballroom, free parking. Tel (0624) 624540. See page 40

CORNAA GUESTHOUSE, 46 Murray's Road, Douglas. Cornaa is a small, friendly house, under the personal supervision of the proprietor. Facilities include tea/coffee making trays, shaving points in all rooms. A bath and shower, TV lounge, B&B and Evening Meals available. Reasonable tariffs. Children welcome. Open all year. 1 crown approved. Tel (0624) 676927

CUNARD HOTEL, 28/29 Loch Prom, Douglas. Friendly, family run private hotel. Full central heating, most bedrooms have en-suite bathrooms/showers, TVs with satellite, radio, tea/coffee making facilities; varied menus, bar and games room. Write or phone for free brochure to Mrs G A Quirk on (0624) 676728. See page 41

DUDLEY HOUSE, 22/24 Christian Road, Douglas. B&B, Dinner and B&B, or self-catering accommodation available. All bedrooms en-suite, colour TV, heating, tea/coffee making facilities. All flats fully self-contained and equipped. Licensed bar, games room, friendly atmosphere. Tel (0624) 676771

ELLAN VANNIN, 31 Loch Promenade, Douglas. Colour TV lounge. Snooker room. Full central heating. Coin operated laundry facilities. Non-smoking dining room. Most bedrooms en-suite. Tea/coffee making facilities. Colour TV in all bedrooms. Private telephones. Radio/roomcall. Tel/Fax (0624) 674824. See page 41

EMPRESS HOTEL, Central Promenade, Douglas. 5 crowns, highly commended hotel, conveniently situated. La Brasserie restaurant. 102 luxurious en-suite rooms with marble bathrooms. Colour teletext TV with satellite and pay-movie channel, telephone, radio, tea/coffee making facilities. Health club. Entertainment. Open all year. Tel (0624) 661155. See page 52

ERINBRAE, Queens Promenade, Douglas. A small friendly 3 crowns private hotel (unlicensed). Ideal for the quieter type of holiday. Seafront position. Easy parking. Close to Summerland, the horse tram terminus and electric railway. En-suite, TV, tea and Coffee making facilities. Tel. (0624) 620829. Fax (0624) 626242

'FERNLEIGH' Palace Road, Douglas. Family run Victorian house. Parking, garage, garden, comfortable en-suite & economy bedrooms with tea making facilities, radio & TV. B&B from £15 daily. Enquiries to Jennifer Hall. Tel (0624) 675553.

GLEN MONA GUEST HOUSE, 6 Mona Drive, Douglas. Comfortable family run guest house 40 yards from a sandy beach. Heating and tea/coffee making facilities in all rooms. Licensed Bar. TV Lounge. Children welcome. B&B from £13.50. B&B and Evening Meal from £18.00. Bar meals and packed lunches available. Tel (0624) 676755.

HAMPTON MANOR, Old Castletown Road, Port Soderick. Tastefully furnished country house. B&B (full English breakfast). Set in 3 acres. Magnificent views. Ample parking. 5 minutes to shore. 3 miles to Douglas. Golf courses close by. Tel (0624) 621539

"HIGH STANDING", Main Road, Baldrine. "High Standing" is a small highly commended family run Bed & Breakfast establishment with all bedrooms en-suite and enjoying TV, Radio and Tea/Coffee facilities. Sea and country views, 10 minutes drive to Douglas. Tel (0624) 861220

IMPERIAL HOTEL, Central Promenade, Douglas. Ideally situated, family run hotel. 63 comfortable bedrooms, many en-suite, with TV, heating, tea/coffee making facilities, intercom and radio. 2 lifts. Entertainment and dancing. Bar. TV room, night porter, laundry facilities, sunbed. Tel (0624) 621656. See page 47

MELROSE PRIVATE HOTEL, 14 Loch Promenade, Douglas. Close to all amenities. All bedrooms are en-suite with tea/coffee making facilities, TV, radio and hairdryer. Ironing room. Baby facilities. Open all year. Choice of menus. Bar open until midnight. Contact Keith & Angela. Tel (0624) 676265. See page 41

"MISTRAL", Hilltop Rise, Farmhill, Braddan. Bed & Breakfast from £15. TV, tea/coffee facilities in bedrooms. Pleasant lounge and garden overlooking fields and hills. 5 minutes drive from Douglas. Isle of Man Tourist Board listed commended. Open all year. Mrs Sheila Wilson. Tel (0624) 662827.

NO 2 VICTORIA PLACE, DOUGLAS. Newly restored period townhouse in quiet central situation close to shops, promenade, theatre and museum. Open 12 months. Tourist Board Rating 4 keys Commended. Seasonal tariff up to 4 people £197-305 pw inc fuel charges (based on 3 weeks). Tel (0624) 620362 or write 'In Town Locations', TJC Barker, 50 Derby Square, Douglas, Isle of Man, IM1 3LP.

PALACE HOTEL, Central Promenade, Douglas. Centrally located on the majestic curve of Douglas Bay. On site facilities include 2 public casinos, nightclub, 2 cinemas, health club, leisure club. Travel inclusive packages. Tel (0624) 662662. See page 44

PITCAIRN PRIVATE HOTEL, 2 Church Road Marina, Douglas. The hotel is situated close to many amenities under the personal supervision of proprietors. Heating and tea making facilities available all bedrooms. En-suite rooms available. Tourist Board grading 2 crowns approved. Tel (0624) 674771

RIO HOTEL, Loch Promenade, Douglas. Beautiful sea views, near shops & amenities. Cocktail lounge. Most rooms en-suite, all rooms have radio/TV inc satellite, tea/coffee making facilities; home cooked food with varied breakfast menu; non-smoking dining room; laundry facilities; bar meals and snacks. Tel (0624) 623491. See page 51

SILVERCRAIGS HOTEL Queens Promenade Douglas. Superbly situated close to all amenities and opposite the beach. Hotel of high reputation for service and excellent cuisine. Open all the year. Full central heating. All bedrooms with en-suite facilities. Tel (0624) 674903. See page 53

SILVER JUBILEE GUESTHOUSE, 28 Castlemona Avenue, Douglas. Coloured TVs and tea making facilities all rooms. B&B £11. Evening meal (optional) £4. Close to sea front on level ground. TV lounge, large dining room. Open May-Sept. Tel (0624) 676011

WINDSOR HOTEL, Loch Promenade, Douglas. Situated on sea front, enjoying splendid views of Douglas Bay. Also adjacent to main shopping area, theatres, etc. Good Food. Coffee Shop. Lift. Night Porter. Travel package. Enquiries to A D Creevy (0624) 676169. See page 51

ONCHAN

PARK HOTEL, 1-3 Royal Avenue, Port Jack, Onchan. Ideally situated, most bedrooms enjoying spectacular views. Well appointed hotel with full central heating, direct dial telephones, radio room call and satellite TV. Cocktail bar, garden lounge and Regency Restaurant. Tel (0624) 676906. See page 98

PEEL

BALLACALLIN COUNTRY PUB & HOTEL, Dalby. Comfortable/modern en-suite accommodation with TV/Tea & Coffee making facilities. Also morning coffee, lunches, afternoon teas, evening meals. Tel (0624) 842030. See page 75

CUMMAL CHEH, 25 Douglas Street, Peel. Homestay scheme. Bed & Breakfast, evening meal negotiable. 1 double bedroom. Central heating, shower and bath available. Cot available for 1 baby. Close to shops and beach. Beverage-making facilities in room. Malcolm and Karen Jackson. Tel (0624) 842793

FERNLEIGH PRIVATE HOTEL, Marine Parade, Peel. Standard to en-suite bedrooms, all being heated and tastefully decorated, tea/coffee trays. First class breakfast and dinner menu, plus vegetarian food. Ideally situated. Car parking. Low cost travel packages can be arranged. Contact June or David Pownall. Tel (0624) 842435.

"SEABOURNE HOUSE", Mount Morrison, Peel. Friendly guesthouse, beautiful views across bay and castle. Central heating. Colour TV and refreshments in all rooms. Parking, Bus Route, Shops, Laundry nearby. £15 B&B May-Sept (TT Fortnight £18 B&B) £12.50 Oct-April. Open all year. Holiday flatlet available £150 weekly. Tel (0624) 842571

THE HAVEN, 10 Peveril Avenue, Peel. Homely guesthouse. Non-smoking. Superior en-suite accommodation. CTV. Tea/coffee facilities. Central heating. Close to amenities. Lovely views. Parking. Evening Meals. Bed & Breakfast from £15 pp. 3 crowns, highly commended. Phone Anthea for accommodation, air/sea package Travel Services ATOL 1965. (0624) 842585

SULBRICK FARMHOUSE, St Marks. Stay in our traditional Manx farmhouse. Open April-October. Situated in the peaceful countryside. Ideal for ramblers – yet only 15 mins drive from Douglas and Castletown. Bed & Breakfast from £12. Guests' TV lounge. Tea/coffee facilities. Children welcome. Tel (0624) 851248

PORT ERIN

BALMORAL HOTEL, Promenade, Port Erin. 2 crowns commended. A friendly beachfront hotel. Excellent reputation for good food. Close to all amenities, licensed, en-suites available. B&B from £17 pp per night. Ideal base for walkers. Evening meals available. Tel (0624) 833126. Fax (0624) 835343

CHERRY ORCHARD HOTEL, Bridson Street, Port Erin. Ideally situated; well appointed hotel including fully maintained self-catering apartments. In-house leisure facilities; excellent cuisine. Travel inclusive offers. Tel Freephone 0800 833627. See page 71

FALCON'S NEST HOTEL, Family run hotel with A la Carte Restaurants, a simple bar lunch or Sunday Carvery. Open all year round. Real Ales, Food and real atmosphere. Tel (0624) 834077. See page 67

GROSVENOR HOTEL, The Promenade, Port Erin. Tel (0624) 834124. Renowned for its cleanliness, friendliness and excellent cuisine. Colour TVs and teamakers in all bedrooms. Many en-suites available. Licensed bar and games rooms. Open all year. Child free offers. B&B from £15.50. Evening meal £7.50. Senior citizen reduction. 2 crowns approved.

PROMENADE BED & BREAKFAST, York House, The Promenade, Port Erin. 18 bedrooms, 2 lounges, lecture room, close amenities, shops, transport, catering, etc. All guests welcome including societies, divers, golfers, environmentalists, etc. Excellent food including vegetarian. Pets welcome. Open all year. B&B from £12.95 pp. En-suite available. Tel/Fax (0624) 832440

THE PORT ERIN HOTELS. A selection of 5 quality hotels located in the beautiful resort of Port Erin. Our hotels are tailored for the discerning visitor with an appreciation of beauty, peace and tranquillity. Each hotel has every modern facility needed by the holidaymaker. Tel (0624) 833558. See page 70

RAMSEY AND THE NORTH

GRAND ISLAND HOTEL, Ramsey. The island's only 4 star hotel on one of Europe's finest sites enjoying panoramic views. 54 bedrooms including 8 suites. Extensive indoor leisure centre. 6 croquet lawns and 1 putting green. Nearby horse riding, golf, fishing and shooting. High quality cuisine with choice of restaurants and informal bar meals. Tel (0624) 812455. See page 90 & 92

ROSE COTTAGE, St Judes, Nr Ramsey. B&B from £22. Evening meal £10/12. 3 crowns commended. All rooms en-suite, colour TV, tea/coffee maker, adjustable C/H, large garden, sun room, private parking.
Tel (0624) 880610

THALLOO-REE, Dhoon, Maughold. Bed & Breakfast. Modern bungalow in picturesque setting, sea view overlooking glen between Laxey and Ramsey. Convenient to bus and tram. Twin en-suite room. Central heating. Own lounge with TV. £16.50 pp. Commended. Proprietor: Mrs Hazel Lace. Tel (0624) 861450

"THE SULBY GLEN HOTEL", Sulby Straight, Nr Ramsey. Traditional country inn, fully centrally heated with licensed bars and private car park. Meals available every lunch and evening with a bistro 4 nights a week. Most rooms are en-suite with TV and tea/coffee making facilities. Pub entertainment some nights. 2 crowns approved. RAC listed. BSH approved. Tel (0624) 897240

SELF CATERING

BALLACARNANE FARM BUNGALOW, Michael. Spacious bungalow, to sleep 10, with panoramic views. Family room with colour TV; large lounge with dining facilities; 5 bedrooms, bathroom, shower room; kitchen with freezer, fridge, dishwasher, microwave, split-level electric cooker; utility room with sink, washing machine and tumbler drier; gas central heating; parking for several cars. Tel (0624) 878261 See page 82

CHERRY ORCHARD HOTEL, Bridson Street, Port Erin. Ideally situated; well appointed en-suite rooms or fully maintained self-catering apartments. In-house leisure facilities; excellent cuisine. Travel inclusive offers. Tel Freephone 0800 833627. See page 71

CHERRY TREE HOUSE, Port St Mary. Charming new property, 3 bedrooms, with lovely views towards the hills and Colby. Beautifully furnished. Close to local shops. Half a mile to local Golf Course. Welcome food pack included in price. From £220 per week. Contact

Classified Accommodation

Mike or Carol Quirk on (0624) 834932/833502 or write to 'Estoril', Ballakeyll, Colby, Isle of Man.

CREGGAN MOAR FARMHOUSE, Dalby, Peel. Self-catering house in secluded situation in lovely glen on beautiful west coast with own beach. Modernised and fully equipped for 7 people (4 bedrooms), bathroom, shower room, fitted kitchen and large lounge. 5 keys commended. Tel (0624) 843539. Fax (0624) 844204.

CREGLEA FARM COTTAGE, Dalby. Well equipped s/c cottage on west coast working farm. Magnificent views to the Calf. Sleeps 4, 2 bedrooms, all bed/table linen and towels provided. Gas C/H and Elec included. Regret no pets. 4 keys. Highly commended. Tel (0624) 842535 or 823506. Fax (0624) 824674

"HIGHVIEW", 2 Bradda Mount, Bradda East, Port Erin. Self catering holiday home. Excellent sea views. 3 double beds. 2 single beds. Teletext TV. Gas central heating and all electricity included in rent. Payphone. Cot and high chair. Automatic washer, tumble drier, microwave. Full details on application.
Tel Mr P Rigby (0772) 743924

ISLE OF MAN, Port St Mary. A beautifully renovated stone cottage. Lovely views. Sleeps 4. 2 bedrooms, both en-suite. Colour TV/video, dishwasher, washing machine, fridge, gas central heating. For further details telephone (0624) 832568.

KIONSLIEU FARM COTTAGES, Kionslieu Farm, Higher Foxdale. Newly-built or renovated farm buildings, set in peaceful countryside. Spacious, centrally-heated cottages. Fully equipped including linen and towels. Farm animals and rural views. Tel (0624) 801349. See page 76

MANX COTTAGE. Situated Old Laxey, close to Harbour, Wheel, MER Station. Fully equipped. Colour TV, microwave, fridge, etc. Linen provided. Lounge, kitchen, shower. 2 bedrooms. Sleeps 3. Pets welcome. Open 12 months. Reductions for long lets. Tariff from £150 pw, inc gas central heating. 3 keys commended. Tel (0624) 672056

RONAGUE HOLIDAY HOMES. Architect converted country Methodist Chapel in open countryside, 2 bedrooms, splendid views, garden. Manx farm house in own land, 3 bedrooms, private with lovely views. Both convenient for all southern towns. 10 minutes from airport. Tel (0624) 823355.

SHENVALLEY COTTAGE, Patrick, Nr Peel. 4 keys commended, self catering, 2 bedroomed beamed cottage. Sleeps 4. Comfortable, fully equipped, double-glazed in quiet area with beautiful views. Garden and private parking. 1.5 miles from Peel. Sorry no pets. Tel (0624) 801674.

STANLEY HOUSE HOLIDAY APARTMENTS, Marine Parade, Peel. Self catering accommodation situated on the seafront overlooking the bay and Peel Castle. 5 mins walk from the town amenities. You can relax on the sandy beach across the road from us. Free parking. Tel (0624) 842198 or write to M F Le Moignan, Stanley House, 3 Marine Parade, Peel, Isle of Man.

CARAVANS & CAMPING

GLENLOUGH FARM CAMPSITE. Open May-October, sheltered site on TT course. On main bus route Douglas to Peel. Flush toilets, wash-hand basins, hot and cold water, showers, electricity and power points, telephone. Everyone welcome. Tel (0624) 851326

EATING OUT

BALLACALLIN COUNTRY PUB & HOTEL, Dalby. Free House. Lunchtime & Evening Meals served every day. Morning Coffees and Afternoon Teas. Traditional Sunday Lunch and Bar Meals served on Sundays between 12 noon & 3 pm. Also comfortable, modern en-suite accommodation with TV/Tea & Coffee making facilities. Tel (0624) 842030. See page 74

FALCON'S NEST HOTEL, Family run hotel with A la Carte Restaurants, a simple bar lunch or Sunday Carvery. Open all year round. Real Ales, Food and real atmosphere. Tel (0624) 834077. See page 67

LA ROSETTE RESTAURANT, Ballasalla. Egon Ronay Starred. Chef Patron. Lunch: Tuesday-Saturday 12 noon-2.00pm; Evening: Tuesday-Saturday 7.00-10.00pm. Tel (0624) 822940. See page 58

PEPPERMILL RESTAURANT, Sulby Mill. Lunch 12 to 3 pm. Dinner 6 to 10 pm. Open 7 days & 7 nights a week. Licensed. Tel (0624) 897436. See page 132

RUSHEN ABBEY HOTEL, Ballasalla. Lunches served 6 days a week 12-2 pm. Reasonable prices, varied menu. Snacks and tea/coffee served all day. Friendly atmosphere. Children welcome. Live music every Saturday. Tel (0624) 823240. See page 58

SARTFIELD FARMHOUSE, Barre Garrow. Licensed restaurant and cafe. Good farmhouse fare in friendly surroundings. Meals, snacks, afternoon tea, A la Carte. Open every day. Tel (0624) 878280. See page 84

INDEX

(Numbers in *italic* refer to illustrations)

A
Abbeylands 112
Adjacent Islands 4, 18, 24
Algare Hill 112
Andreas 86, 132
Anglo-Saxons 18, 86
Aquadrome 43
Arbory 74
Arboretum 33
Ayre – Point of 16, 29, 30, 90, 100, 104, 116
Ayres 26, 120

B
Baldrine 10, 111, 130, 134, 138
Baldwin 31, 112, 122
Ballabeg 74, 138
Ballacarnane 104
Ballacraine 114
Ballafesson 125
Ballaglass 111
Ballajora 10, 109, 138
Ballakillowey 125
Ballaragh 134
Ballasalla 56, 59, 124, 128, 139
Ballaugh 10, 33, 84, 85, 86, 114
Ballure 88
Banks 54, 59, 64, 72, 80, 94, 96
Barregarrow 122
Barrule – North 10, 110, 132
Barrule – South 10, 21, 128, 132
Bay Fine 24
Bay ny Carrickey 24, 64, 104, 128
Bishops 10, 20, 21, 22, 29, 62, 63, 84, 87, 88
Bligh – Captain 97
Block Eary 132
Blue Point 26
Bradda 24, 125
Bradda Head 24, 71, 74, 144
Braddan 144
Braaid – The 128, 129
Brandywell 109, 114, 122, 131
Bride 86, 87, 116, 117, 132
British Government 10, 22
Building Societies 54, 94
Bungalow – The 118, 131
Burroo – The 27

C
Caley – Arthur 150
Calf of Man 26, 27, 59, 67, 74, 248
Captain of the Parish 104
Castletown 10, 24, 29, 59, 61, 63, 64, 102, 123, 124, 139
Castle Rushen 21, 62, 63, 74, 88

Cathedral 10, 29, 77
Celtic 10, 27, 77
Celts 18
Chasms 24, 67
Chicken Rock 27
Christian – Sir Hugh 59
Christian – Fletcher 97
Christian – William 21, 22, 59, 63
Christianity 12, 20, 26, 27, 77, 84
Chronicon Manniae 56, 88
Cinemas 43, 59
Cistercians 20, 59
Clay Head 26
Coastguard 26, 54
Colby 18, 74, 124
Conister Rock 29
Contrary Head 26
Cornaa 10, 109, 111, 132, 138
Corrany 132
Corrin's Tower 26
Cranstal 26, 102, 104
Cregneash 22, 24, 67, 125, 128
Creg-ny-Baa 109, 131
Creg Willeys Hill 121
Cronkbourne Village 112
Cronk ny Arrey Laa 26, 31
Cronk Sumark 119
Cronk – The 118
Cronk-y-Voddy 121
Crosby 114, 124, 148
Crossag 56
Curraghs 33, 116, 118
Curraghs Wild Life Park 33

D
Dalby 74, 75, 128
Deemster 19, 81
Derbyhaven 24, 29, 59, 60, 102, 147
Devil's Elbow 104
Dhoon 26, 111, 132, 134
Distances 37, 38, 56, 61, 65, 68, 77, 88, 95, 108, 112, 114, 121, 125, 130
Dollagh Mooar 118
Douglas 9, 10, 12, 16, 18, 24, 26, 29, 31, 32, 33, 38, 39, 40, 41, 43, 45, 47, 49, 51, 53, 58, 98, 100, 102, 108, 109, 111, 112, 114, 128, 130, 134, 136, 138
Dreemskerry 10, 138
Druidale 114

E
Eairy Dam – The 126, 128
England 10, 18, 20, 21, 22, 23, 24, 31, 109, 116, 120
Ellan Vannin 23, 31, 35, 84, 90, 116, 128, 146
Events Calendar 106, 107, 145
Eyreton 114

F
Fairies 148
Fairy Bridge 148

Fairy Cottage 10, 111, 130, 138
Fenella's Beach 27
Fistard 67
Fort Island 29
Foxdale 10, 58, 75, 76, 124, 128, 140

G
Gaiety Theatre 16, 43
Gansey 64, 104
Garey 128
Garwick 102, 111
Glens 24, 31, 32, 33, 74, 82, 96, 104, 114, 116, 118, 132
138
Glen Maye 20, 74, 128
Glen Roy 131
Glen Vine 114
Gob ny Ushtey 26
Gooseneck – The 132
Governors 10
  Horton 29
  Loch 16, 22, 41
  Smelt 62, 63
Greeba 31, 113, 114
Groudle 10, 26, 102, 111, 130, 134, 138
Groudle Railway 102, 111, 134

H
Hango Hill 22, 23, 63
Hibernian – The 132
Hilary – Sir Wiliam 29, 150
Hope – The 124
Horse Trams 9, 136
Hospital – Noble's 54
Hospital – Ramsey Cottage 92
House of Keys 22, 34, 62, 63, 81
Howe – The 67, 125

I
Injebreck 31, 32, 112, 114, 124
Ireland 10, 18, 20, 24, 37, 109, 120
Isle of Man Steam Packet 9, 12, 16, 35, 37, 38
Isle of Man Railways 9, 10, 31, 49, 56, 69, 96, 118, 138, 139, 140
Isle of Man Government 32, 33, 41, 47, 53, 100, 124, 136, 139
Isle of Man Department of Tourism, Leisure & Transport 14, 15, 106, 107

J
Jurby 12, 18, 20, 86, 118

K
Kate's Cottage 109
Keeills 29, 148
Kentraugh 64
Kings and Queens
  Alexander III 148
  Arthur 128
  Atholl – Dukes of 10, 22, 38, 59
  Charles I 21

Index

Charles II 21
Crovan 20, 88
Derby – Earls of 21, 29, 59, 63
Edward III 10
Edward VIII 12, 38
Elizabeth I 63
Elizabeth II 80
George III 22
George IV 22
George V 38
Henry IV 10
Henry VI 77
Henry VIII 150
Magnus 56
Olaf 88
Orkney – Earls of 20
Orry 20, 59, 134
Reginald II 56
Victoria 12, 16, 23, 38
Kermode – William 72
Kermode – Robert Quayle 72
Kewaigue 51, 128
Kerroodhoo 75
Kewley – "Dawsey" 38
Kione ny Cleigh 26
Kirk Michael 10, 26, 82, 84, 104, *114*
Kitterland 27

L

Lace – John 150
Langness 29, 59, *99*
Laxey 9, 10, 26, 33, 59, 61, *95*, *102*, 109, 111, 120, 130, *131*, 134, 138, *139*
Laxey Wheel 9, 96
Leisure Centres 54, 59, 64, 94
Lhen – The 20, 116, 118
Liargee Frissel 116
Little London 121, 122
Loaghtan – Sheep 27
Lonan 111, 130
London 22

M

MacCoole – Finn 18, 24
Magnetic Hill 140
Manx Airlines 35, 37
Manx National Heritage 96, 141, 146
Manx National Trust 24, 26, 67
Maughold 26, 92, 102, 109, 110, *149*
Milky Way 20
Milner 24, 26
Milntown 20
Mining 9, 75, 95, 96, 124
Mooragh Park 33, 90, *94*, 102, 116, 120
Mountains 20, 31, 33, 58, 81, 114, 116, 122, 131, 132, 148
Mull Peninsula 18, 24, 65, 67, 71, 128
Museums 10, 38, 62, 63, 67, 74, 77, 139, *141,* 142, 143
Mylchreests Drives 108 – 134

N

Nab – The 114
Niarbyl 26, 27, *28*, 74, *76,* 128
Noble – Henry Bloom 33
Normans 35
Northern Ireland 10, 24, 71, 109, 120, 122
Norway 10, 18, 20, 21

O

Onchan 10, 26, 33, 38, 97, 98, 102, 130, 132, 138

P

Parishes 12, 21, 34, 56, 61, 64, 74, 81, 84, 86, 124
Parks 32, 33
Peel 10, 18, 26, 27, 31, 77, *79, 80,* 100, 104, 114, 121, *122,* 124, 140
Peel Castle 21, 26, 27, *28,* 148
Perwick 65, 67
Pixton – Captain 122
Port Cornaa 111
Port-e-Chee 112
Port Erin 10, 18, 24, *25,* 26, 27, 67, *68,* 71, 72, *73,* 100, *103,* 104, 125, 128, 139
Port e Vullen 102
Port Jack 26, 102, 130, 134
Port Lewaigue 102
Port Mooar 26, 109
Port St Mary 10, 18, 24, 26, 65, *66,* 67, 104, 139
Poyll Vaaish 18, 24, 63
Public Amenities 54, 59, 64, 67, 72, 80, 92, 96

Q

Quakers 26, 111
Quarter Bridge 114
Quilliam – Captain John 63, 74, 150

R

Ramsey 10, 26, 32, 33, 88, *89,* 90, 92, *93,* 102, 104, 106, *109,* 116, 120, 132, 138, 140
Reeves – Lieut Edward 97
RNLI 29, 150
Romans 18, 35, 146
Ronaldsway 24, 59
Rushen Abbey 20, 56, 58

S

Santon 128
Sarah's Cottage 121
Sartfell 18, 122
Scarlett 18, 62
Scotland 10, 18, 20, 21, 23, 24, 109, 120, 122
Shakespeare – William 77
Sharks 24
Sheadings 34, 56, 86, 125
Signpost Corner 108
Silverdale 58, 124
Slogh – The 125, 128
Snaefell 9, 10, 12, 18, 31, 63, 109, 118, 138
Social Cottage 131
Sound – The 24, 67, 100, 104, *127,* 128
Spanish Head 24, 26, 67
Spanish Armada 24
Stanley – House of 10, 21, 22, 27, 74
Stevenson 63
St Johns 10, 33, 34, 80, 114, *121,* 124, 140
St Judes 132
St Luke's 112
St Mark's 124
St Michael 29
St Patrick 10, 26, 27, 77
St Trinians 114
Strandhall 64
Strang – The 114
Strathallan 136
Sulby 10, 12, 18, 88, 118, 132, *133*
Sulby Claddaghs 118
Sulby Cossacks 132
Sulby Reservoir 118, *120,* 132
Summerland 43
Surnames – Manx 18, 20

T

Thing 20
Tholt-e-Will 118, 132
Three Legs of Man 148
Tourist Information 47, 51, 54, 64, 72, 80, 94, 96, 102
Tower of Refuge 16
Trinian St
TT Races 9, 16, 41, 49, 95, 108, 109, 114, 120, 121, *131*, 132, 138
Tynwald 10, 11, 20, 22, 33, 34, 81, 82, 112, 124
Tynwald Hill 10, 34, 81, 124
Tynwald Mills 82, 114, 120

U

Union Mills 114

V

Villa Marina 33
Vikings 10, 18, 20, 29, 34, 59, 86, 95, 118

W

Wales 10, 18, 24, 109
Wesley – John 62
Walker – Sir Baldwin 150

158 Discount Vouchers

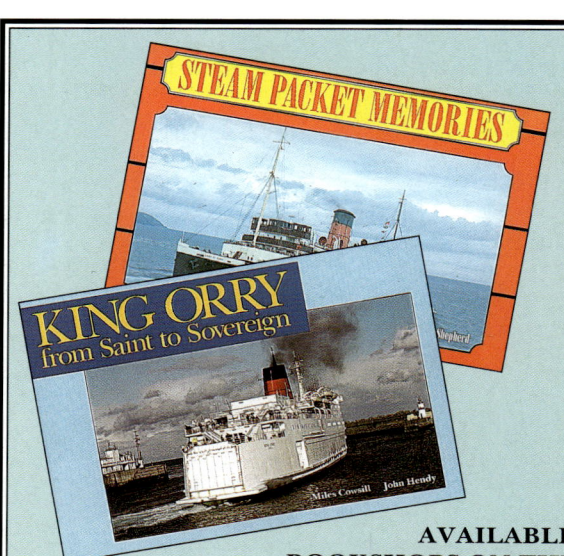

STEAM PACKET MEMORIES
by John Sheppard
Forty eight pages of pure nostalgia dealing with the last 25 years of the much-loved Manx turbine steamers. Authoritative account by former employee, acknowledged authority and fleet expert. Price £3.45

KING ORRY From Saint to Sovereign
by Miles Cowsill & John Hendy
The story of the Steam Packet's multi-purpose ferry explaining why she was built, the problems with her construction and the years as the train ferry Saint Eloi. The history comes right up to date when the ship is Monarch of the Irish Sea. 48 pages. Colour and Black & White photos. Price: £3.45

AVAILABLE FROM ALL LEADING BOOKSHOPS ON THE ISLE OF MAN OR FROM
Ferry Publications
12 Millfields Close, Pentlepoir, Kilgetty, Pembrokeshire, SA68 0SA.
Tel: 0834 813991

BÉZIER DESIGN LIMITED

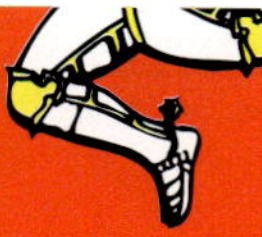

Traditional creative skills
linked with contemporary
production methods

CAMROSE HOUSE · 106 MAIN STREET · PEMBROKE SA71 4HN
TELEPHONE 0646 686418 · FAX 0646 686309 · COMPUSERVE 100014, 2300

Ballacallin Country Pub & Hotel
Dalby

£1 off Full Sunday Lunch

per person on production of this voucher
Reservations Tel: 842030
Traditional Sunday lunch served between
12 noon and 3pm
VISIT THE WEST OF THE ISLAND

SPECIAL OFFER

The story of the famous Isle of Man TT Races
"You couldn't do it now!" for only £6.95 inc.
post & packing (normal price £8.00).
Send cheque or postal order along with your
name and address to:
**CELT MARKETING & RESEARCH,
ABBEY FORD, BALLASALLA, ISLE OF MAN**
(see ad on page 33 for more details)

ACKNOWLEDGMENTS

The Publishers would like to thank the Honourable Alan Bell MHK, Minister of the Isle of Man Department of Tourism, Leisure and Transport, for writing the foreword to this publication. Our thanks also go to Terry Toohey, Chief Executive of the Isle of Man Department of Tourism, Leisure and Transport, Malcolm Connor, Director of Marketing and Geof Burnett, Chairman of the Tourism Marketing Committee, for their support and valuable assistance.

The Directors of Lily Publications would like to express their gratitude to Ian Smith and Joy Sandifer of Bézier Design for handling all the design work for this Isle of Man 1994-5 Approved Publication in such an efficient and professional manner. The Publishers would also like to thank the following for their assistance:

Mike Bathgate (Manx Airlines), Stephen Beevers (Isle of Man Treasury), Ian and Monica Clark (Island Photographics), Doreen Douglas (Celt Marketing and Research), Ann Faragher (Department of Tourism), John Hendy, Henk van der Lugt, Richard Kirkman (Isle of Man Steam Packet Company Limited), Annie Lowey (Ronague Enterprises Limited), Dave Moore (Gauntlet Productions), Andrew Pennington, Nigel Rotheroe (Crossleys, Accountants), Pat Somner (Lily Publications), Graham Warhurst and Paul Ogden (Isle of Man Railways), Doctor Brian Stowell (Isle of Man Department of Education), Noel and Mary Cringle, Jean Wilson and all our Advertisers for their generosity.

PUBLISHERS: Lily Publications (Isle of Man)
DESIGNERS: Bézier Design Limited
REPRO: Haven Colourprint
PRINTING: Harcourt Litho, Swansea
PHOTOGRAPHY: All pictures unless credited are the work of Miles Cowsill – Lily Publications (Isle of Man)

Discount Vouchers

10% off any Manx-made Pipe

On production of this voucher at:
LAXEY PIPES, THE QUAY, OLD LAXEY. TELEPHONE: 861074

Valid during 1994-95 only. Not refundable as cash.

The Peppermill Restaurant

Free Glass of Wine

On presentation of this voucher when you purchase a meal.

Not refundable as cash. Valid until end 1994.

SPECIAL OFFER

The story of the famous Isle of Man TT Races *"You couldn't do it now!"* for only £6.95 inc. post & packing (normal price £8.00). Send cheque or postal order along with your name and address to:

CELT MARKETING & RESEARCH, ABBEY FORD, BALLASALLA, ISLE OF MAN

(see ad on page 33 for more details)

**Ballacallin Country Pub & Hotel
Dalby**

£1 off Full Sunday Lunch

per person on production of this voucher
Reservations Tel: 842030
Traditional Sunday lunch served between 12 noon and 3pm

VISIT THE WEST OF THE ISLAND

LILY PUBLICATIONS

 Photography

 Publishers

 Printing & Design

Lily Publications (Isle of Man),
PO Box 1, Portland House, Station Road, Ballasalla, Isle of Man
Tel: (0624) 823644
UK Office: 12 Millfields Close, Kilgetty, Pembrokeshire, Wales, SA68 0SA.
Tel: (0834) 811895 Fax: (0834) 814484